W9-BRK-392

A Study Guide Based on the Book

Daughters

of Eve

WOMEN OF
THE BIBLE
SPEAK TO
WOMEN
OF TODAY

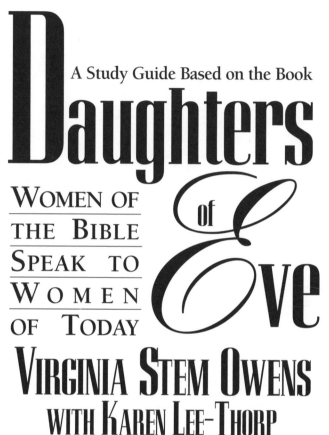

VIRGINIA STEM OWENS
WITH KAREN LEE-THORP

NAVPRESS
BRINGING TRUTH TO LIFE
NavPress Publishing Group
P.O. Box 35001, Colorado Springs, Colorado 80935

The Navigators is an international Christian organization. Jesus Christ gave His followers the Great Commission to go and make disciples (Matthew 28:19). The aim of The Navigators is to help fulfill that commission by multiplying laborers for Christ in every nation.

NavPress is the publishing ministry of The Navigators. NavPress publications are tools to help Christians grow. Although publications alone cannot make disciples or change lives, they can help believers learn biblical discipleship, and apply what they learn to their lives and ministries.

Cover illustration: Cindy Lindgren

Scripture quotations in this publication are taken from the *HOLY BIBLE: NEW INTERNATIONAL VERSION*® (NIV®), copyright © 1973, 1978, 1984 by International Bible Society, used by permission of Zondervan Publishing House, all rights reserved; and the *King James Version* (KJV).

Printed in the United States of America

1 2 3 4 5 6 7 8 9 10 11 12 13 14 15 / 99 98 97 96 95

Published in association with
the literary agency of Alive Communications,
P.O. Box 49068, Colorado Springs, CO 80949.

CONTENTS

HOW TO USE THIS GUIDE 5

1
Mothers
MARY, THE MOTHER OF JESUS 7

2
Women and Marriage
MICHAL 19

3
Women on the Outside
WOMAN WITH THE ISSUE OF BLOOD 29

4
Single Women
MARTHA 37

5
Women and Violence
RIZPAH 49

6
Sensual Women
MARY OF BETHANY 57

7
Manipulative Women
REBEKAH 63

8
Political Women
JEZEBEL 73

9
Business Women
SAPPHIRA 83

10
Women and the Supernatural
THE NECROMANCER OF ENDOR 91

HOW TO USE THIS GUIDE

*I*n the past few decades we've come to realize our distance from biblical women. The details of their world—drawing water at the town well, arranged marriages based primarily on economics, gauging worth by childbearing—all make their lives seem not only ancient but alien to us. Can these women have anything significant to tell us today?

How much has life really changed for women? Are we, even after centuries of change, still "sisters under the skin" with the Middle Eastern, North African, and Mediterranean women who people the biblical pages? Do their fears and sorrows, hopes and joys connect with ours? If we paid attention to them—not as cultural oddities or bit players in the biblical drama—would they have anything significant to say to us?

The book *Daughters of Eve* recounts the stories of thirty biblical women. This discussion guide is a companion to that book. Ten women's stories have been selected for you to reflect upon with a group. You don't have to read the book in order to use this guide because each discussion session includes an excerpt from the book.

Because most of us have busy schedules, this guide has been designed so that as participants you don't have to prepare anything in advance of your discussion sessions. During the discussions, you can jot your thoughts and responses in this guide. Alternatively, your group may agree to read the text and answer the questions in advance of your discussion.

Each session contains the following elements:

Scripture Passages. The verse references at the beginning of each session indicate the passages that tell one woman's story. If you are preparing in advance, you may find it helpful to read these passages on your own. If you are not preparing in advance, your group leader may select one or more of these passages for the group to read together. It is not absolutely necessary to read all of the designated passages because they are summarized in the text that follows. In some cases the book *Daughters of Eve* contains more Scripture references than those listed in this guide.

One Woman's Story. Next you will find the woman's story as told in *Daughters of Eve.* In some cases the excerpt is abbreviated from a longer account in the book. If you are preparing in advance, read this story on your own and jot notes to yourself: How does it make you feel? What questions does it raise for you? What do you learn from it? If you are not preparing in advance, your group can plan five to ten minutes for participants to read the story silently.

Your Thoughts. The questions in this guide are intended as ideas to spark discussion. Don't feel you must cover all of them. They offer you a chance to relate your own experience to that of the woman you are studying. If the story prompts other, more pressing questions from participants, you may prefer to pursue those.

Session 1 includes two questions that preceed Mary's story. Since the mother of Jesus has received more attention than any other biblical woman (Eve might be an exception), these questions give participants a chance to discuss what they already know—accurate or inaccurate—about Mary. If group members don't already know each other well, these questions also allow you to introduce yourselves, to tell some of the background you each bring to the group.

The last question in each session invites you to do something active about what you have discussed. Not everyone will see a way to put your insights into practice after every session. However, each session will probably spur some action for someone.

A Response of Prayer. Each session ends with an idea for group prayer. Prayer will be the primary thing you *do* about what you have discussed.

If your group already has a customary way to pray together, you may enjoy adapting some of these ideas as fresh approaches. If participants are not accustomed to praying in groups, you may want to tailor these ideas into a format participants will find comfortable. For example, you could use the ideas as springboards for silent prayer. Or, if you decide to pray aloud, it's not necessary for each person to pray more than one sentence.

More Women. After reading about one biblical mother or one single woman, participants may want to read about other mothers or singles in the book *Daughters of Eve.* Each session lists the names of the other women included in the book.

1
MARY, THE MOTHER OF JESUS
Mothers

Matthew 2:13-23; Mark 3:20-22,31-34;
Luke 1:26-2:20; John 2:1-11, 19:25-27

1. From what sources have you gotten impressions of Mary
   before reading her story in *Daughters of Eve*?

   ☐ Paintings and statues from the Italian Renaissance
   ☐ Christmas pageants
   ☐ The teaching of my church
   ☐ Reading the Bible on my own
   ☐ Reading other books
   ☐ Other sources (name them):

2. What view of Mary did those sources give you?

Mary's Story
EXCERPTED AND ADAPTED FROM *DAUGHTERS OF EVE*, PAGES 27-38.

*M*ary's first appearance in Scripture is a love scene, not a
theological treatise. A young girl in the small country
town of Nazareth, full of life and health, is anticipating her coming

marriage to Joseph, about whom we know little except that he is once called a carpenter. Mary's fiancé, from the picture Matthew gives us, might well have been an older man, seasoned by experience so that he handles difficulties with equanimity. Whether or not Mary was romantically smitten with him, her family probably considered him something of a catch.

At any rate, Mary is alone, possibly daydreaming about the approaching wedding, when she is startled by the sudden arrival of a strange visitor. Did the angel Gabriel appear in a blinding light, beating wings that spanned the room? Probably not, since Luke says the girl was troubled by the angel Gabriel's words, not his appearance. He begins by paying her outrageous compliments: she is "full of grace," he tells her, favored by God, the lucky winner in a sweepstakes she didn't even know she'd entered. No mere mortal in all the Scriptures is ever addressed in such lofty terms. Mary, whose mother had no doubt taught her to beware of flattering words from strange men, "cast in her mind what manner of salutation this should be."[1]

The stranger's next words are even more fantastic, however. Most men bent on seduction would have assured her she had nothing to worry about. This one, on the other hand, predicts she will in fact get pregnant, that the baby will be a boy, and that she should name him Jesus—a common enough name in that day, something like Victor in English. Only this time the content of the name is to be taken seriously. The child really will be victorious, indeed a king, destined to restore her country's throne to its rightful owner.

Well, Mary may be young, but she's not stupid. She brushes aside the stranger's apparent flattery and glittering promises about the future and pulls the conversation firmly back to the present. "Just how do you expect me to believe all that?" she demands. "I'm not even married yet. And I'm not the kind of girl who fools around." The implication is that she doesn't intend to become one either. Having protected her valuable virginity so far, she's not about to jeopardize it now for some stranger's wild promises.

Gabriel is forced at this point to reveal the principal for whom he's acting: not he, but God himself will be her Lover. And, as if recognizing how incredible this explanation sounds, he offers as proof of his promises the news that Mary's elderly cousin Elizabeth, childless throughout a long marriage, is now miraculously six months pregnant herself.

Faced with the stranger's possession of intimate family secrets in specific physiological detail, Mary at last capitulates to Gabriel's wooing. No longer reticent or ironic, not even maidenly demure, Mary surrenders, declaring herself "the slave of the Lord. Let him do with me what he wants."

Gabriel departs and the scene ends so abruptly that the omitted details of this human-divine conception have intrigued us for twenty centuries.

The next we see of Mary, she is hurrying south from Nazareth to visit her cousin in the suburbs of Jerusalem, a trip of several days' duration. She stays three months with Elizabeth until her cousin's child is born. Then she returns to Nazareth, just as her own condition is beginning to show. She must have known that her marriage plans would now be in peril.

Understandably, Joseph has a hard time accepting Mary's story. She's just come back from the big city, and she expects him to believe some tale about a mysterious stranger and his shady promises? He can hardly be expected to go through with the marriage now. In fact, he is on the point of settling with her family, putting the best face he can on the matter, when Mary's stranger shows up in Joseph's own dreams, confirming her story and instructing him to continue with the wedding plans.

Before the baby is born, however, they are forced to leave Mary's hometown of Nazareth. The Romans have directed that a census be taken of the population in the area. Heads of households are required to register at the husband's birthplace—which for Joseph meant Bethlehem. Popular imagination pictures them as travelers, with Mary, heavy with child, on the back of a donkey.

Because Joseph was returning to his hometown, they likely stayed with his family till Mary's embarrassing pregnancy came to term. In those days, the word we translate as "inn" also meant "guest room" or "dining room." Since many Palestinian families lived in lean-tos built at the entrance to limestone caves that pock the hills around Bethlehem, Mary's in-laws, embarrassed by her untimely pregnancy, may well have stuck the visiting couple back in the cave where the animals were kept, their only "guest room." Then again, perhaps her in-laws were not unkind, only poor and cramped for space. At any rate, it is in this dark barn-cave, far from home, that the teenage girl labors to give birth among strangers.

The Christmas cards always clean the scene up, concealing any sign of her struggle, the bloody rags, and discarded placenta. Instead of picturing her with swollen lips and sweat-matted hair, they show Mary serene and sanitary. Yet the cave floor would have been littered with manure and urine-soaked straw, and the feed trough where she laid her baby filled with moldy hay. No doubt the shepherds who found them that night used similar barn-caves themselves, though perhaps not as a nursery.

How did Mary feel as these strange men stood around her gawking? What did she make of their tales about angels singing? And when the sheepherders left, waking the little town with their rowdy excitement, would she have felt vindicated among the strangers who had previously smirked at her own story? She certainly never forgot that night, storing each detail to savor and reflect upon during the days and years that followed.

The new mother has other visitors in Bethlehem. Scholars from the East arrive, bearing gifts for the new baby—gold, some incense, and myrrh: an ointment used to prepare bodies for burial. Strange gifts for an infant. Not very practical. But then what do men—especially academic types—know about babies anyway?

The months go by in Bethlehem. Then, suddenly, Mary finds herself uprooted once more. The visiting scholars, it appears, have unwittingly upset the king with their loose talk about her child. In a fit of paranoid rage, the ruler plans to wipe out the infant population around Bethlehem. The angel warns Joseph that they must escape to Egypt. This time there will be no one to take them in, no way to make a living as immigrants in that foreign country. Now Mary sees the sense in that gift of gold the wise men brought.

After a while, the old king dies, and they are free to return to their native country. This time the angel directs them back to Mary's old hometown of Nazareth. After such a long absence, after such adventures, Mary must have greeted her friends and family again with relief. Such strange things have happened to her since that day the stranger appeared so suddenly before her. Now her family was safe in Nazareth again; maybe they can settle down, establish a routine, take up where they'd left off.

These are the "hidden years" in the life of the family. We don't know much about what went on during this period, though we can infer that Mary's house began to fill with children. At least seven, finally, in all. Besides Jesus, there was James, Joses, Simon, Judas—all named in Matthew's gospel—and at least two sisters.

Thirty years go by during which we see nothing of Mary other than a curious scene Luke records about Jesus at age twelve. All her children were probably grown and some of them married by the time she appears again. She is quite possibly a widow now, since Joseph does not appear again, though the hometown crowd refers to Jesus scornfully as "the carpenter's son"[2] when he tries to preach to them.

Mary, however, is convinced that her eldest son possesses miraculous powers. When they attend a wedding in the next town, Cana, he performs his first miracle at her express request—turning water into wine when the host runs out. At first he resists. In fact, his response to her is testy to the point of rudeness. "Woman," he says, "what have I to do with you?"[3] Then he adds, "It's not my time yet. Don't push it." But with the unflappable maternal faith of a stage mother, she ignores him and instructs the servants to do whatever he tells them. She obviously has no idea how he might bring this off, or even if he wants to. But she has serene confidence in his power to do it. And at this point even Jesus seems unable to oppose her wishes.

His hometown, unfortunately, does not share her confidence. So Mary's son leaves home for good and wanders the countryside with his followers, most of them ragtag fishermen from Capernaum. Now Mary, so willing in her youth, so confident at the Cana wedding, begins to have doubts about this touring miracle business. Realizing that her boy can't attract large crowds without also attracting the notice of the officials, she wonders if her son has lost his mind. Already experts from the temple in Jerusalem are checking him out. And the Romans, she knows, have no qualms about punishing people they see as a threat to the security and peace of the empire. Fearing both for his safety and his sanity, Mary goes after him to bring him home again. Here we have another clue that she is a widow now, since it is her other sons rather than her husband who accompany her on this mission.

Think of the family dynamics at work here as well. With Joseph dead, the oldest son was obliged to take over his responsibilities as head of the family. Working in the carpentry shop is obviously not what Jesus has mapped out for his life's work, however. The brothers next in line, James and Joses, are understandably exasperated with their older sibling. Who does he think he is anyway, running off and leaving them to take care of everything—including their mother? He needs to come back home and take over the family business, they would have complained to their mother, not go running around the countryside, making wild claims and upsetting the authorities. Very possibly there are also younger children, sisters whose wedding dowries depend on their older brother taking a hand in things. Now he's deserted them, leaving James and Joses holding the bag. Well, it isn't fair and he's not going to get away with it—not if they have anything to say about it.

Mary would have seen their point. What mother wouldn't, pulled by the competing needs of her other children? Thus we see her, in this early stage of Jesus' itinerant ministry, entreating her wayward son to come back home, to give up these crazy ambitions, to stop his dangerous talk about kingdoms and rulers. After all, look what's happened to his cousin John already. He's in jail and likely to have his head chopped off any day now for inciting riots.

Jesus, for his part, feels his family has let him down. Though they may only mean to establish an insanity defense in case of his arrest, their claims that he is not in his right mind give the Pharisees and other temple functionaries a weapon to use against him. These Jewish leaders begin to plant doubt in the minds of his followers, saying Jesus is possessed by demons.

Thus when his mother and brothers appear outside the house where Jesus is staying and demand to talk to him, he is well aware of their mission. Having experienced his mother's determined tenacity at Cana, he knows what extreme measures it will take to deter her. He answers his family's request, as he so often answered everyone, with a question: "Who are my mother and my brothers?"[4] Then, as he gestures around the room at his followers, he adds, "These are my mother and brothers."

Mary, no doubt, was dumbfounded. How can he do this to her? This isn't mere adolescent rebellion; this is outright rejection. He might as well say, "Depart from me; I never knew you." She returns to Nazareth, heartbroken.

Reports of her son filter back to Mary there in the backwater town. No doubt she finds it ironic that he consistently extols the fifth commandment, *Honor thy father and mother,* calling the Pharisees hypocrites for ignoring the spirit of the Law by pledging to their favorite charity while refusing to support their aged parents. He tells rich, young executives to take care of their mother and father, but is he following his own advice? Your first duty, he's telling his followers, is to your heavenly Father.

When she hears the next part of this teaching, however, she feels the sword twist: "If any man come to me, and hate not his father, and mother, and wife, and children, and brethren, and sisters, yea, and his own life also, he cannot be my disciple."[5] Strong words. The hardest of all for a mother.

For her part, Mary has never doubted her son's power. She proved that at the wedding in Cana. Surely he knows she's on his side. What she doesn't understand is the purpose of that power. He's not using it to make them rich. He doesn't even seem interested in freeing his people either from the Romans or those bureaucrats in Jerusalem who make their lives so hard here in the provinces. Why not? Wasn't she led to believe that's what would happen by the stranger and the sheepherders and the Eastern academics? It's still a puzzle to her, ponder it as she will.

She has not forgotten how oddly this son came into the world or how his life was mysteriously preserved. Yet long stretches of ordinary life affect our memory of the extraordinary; that sense of heightened reality the angel brought was hard to recreate now. With Joseph no longer around to corroborate those memories, they have slipped away into some dreamlike realm. The others who had been there, who had borne witness to those singular events—the sheepherders, the Eastern scholars—where are they now? All she has now are her squabbling children and these fragile memories.

Then something changes. Maybe Mrs. Zebedee's leaving home to find Jesus on behalf of her own sons gave Mary an idea. Maybe she heard he was surrounding himself with women who were no better than they ought to be and thought she could at least protect him from their wiles. Maybe she got tired of James and Joses bossing her around and constantly criticizing her beloved boy. Maybe she just missed him. We don't know when or how Mary left home.

13

We only know that at one point she decides to follow her eldest son on his pilgrimage to Jerusalem because she is named in all four gospels as being among the women who followed Jesus from Galilee to the cross.

The three synoptic gospels—Mark, Matthew, and Luke—identify her at this point as "Mary the mother of James and Joses" or "Mary the mother of James the less and Joses." Since people had no last names as we know them, they were routinely identified by formulas of relationship—"the son of," "the wife of," etc. Mary's not being identified as "wife of Joseph" is one of the reasons we assume she is now a widow. But why is she no longer identified as she was earlier as "the mother of Jesus"? John's gospel supplies the reason for this switch.

Mary is a widow, dependent now on her other children. She has very possibly risked their displeasure to leave home and follow this son, the troublemaker. Resentful of their older sibling, they are indignant at Mary's willful defiance of propriety and good sense. Let her go traipsing around the countryside if she likes, but don't expect them to welcome her back with open arms when this whole fiasco comes to its disastrous end. *Be it unto me according to thy will*,[6] she'd said to the stranger that day, never dreaming she would lose the very son she'd been given, nor that the ones who came later would reject her.

As Jesus hung on the cross, one of his final acts is to discharge his filial responsibility. He realizes that as eldest son his duty is indeed to provide for his mother. What will happen to her now that the son she's left home for—not once but twice now—is determined to die, leaving her alone and unprotected? His angry brothers may not take her in again. Jesus, therefore, in a mutual-adoption ceremony, bestows the responsibility for his mother's care on John, his best-loved disciple.

"Woman," he calls her again, just as he had at Cana where she had made her untimely claims on him, "behold thy son."[7]

Woman. Ishah. The name of Eve as well as Mary. He was speaking not only to his own mother but to all mothers since the first one. All the children you thought you'd lost—from Abel and Cain to Jesus—they are restored to you. The children on whom you've lavished your love, expended your nights and days, for whom you've given up your own life—here they are. Just as he had called his disciples his kin on that terrible day when he seemed to reject her, he now calls those same disciples her children, the ones she can count on to care for her. *From that hour that disciple took her unto his own home.*[8]

At the very moment Mary needed it most, when the sword was plunged up to its hilt in her heart, watching her son die, she was at last included in that circle of followers he had drawn around himself, a circle she thought had excluded her. But once she followed him, opened to her also.

Therefore, this is not the last we see of Mary. She helps take down her son's battered body from the cross; she is also a witness to his resurrection. She returns to the upper room with the disciples after Jesus' ascension. And she is called once more "Mary the mother of Jesus."

Not only is this son restored to her, however. She has become an evangelist. Because with her among the disciples are her other sons. And how else should these unbelievers, these scoffers, these siblings who would not be reconciled to their brother in life be reunited with him now, except through the good offices of their mother? In fact, it is James, her second son, who becomes the head of the church in Jerusalem, mediating between the Gentile Christians and the conservative Jerusalem Jews. This son Mary would also lose, according to the historian Josephus, martyred for love of his brother and Lord.

But perhaps by then, gaining and losing had all become one to Mary, a part of the bigger picture. The one all mothers struggle to focus on, where joy of conception turns to pain of childbirth, then becomes almost idolatrous joy as their children grow and wax strong in favor with God and man, the pain returning as those children leave home, a loss that can be fully redeemed only within the circle of those who follow Mary's son.

Your Thoughts
3. What did you learn about Mary from this account of her life? Or, what new perspective did you gain?

4. What feelings does Mary's story raise in you?

5. a. In what ways can you identify with Mary's experience of motherhood?

   b. How has your story been different from hers?

Note: Sometimes it's uncomfortable to be a single or infertile woman in a conversation about motherhood. Do you feel this way? If so, it might be enlightening for your group to hear how you feel.

6. What qualities of Mary are worthy of imitation?

7. How do you suppose you would react if you had to watch your child die for God? (For instance, would you be angry at God?)

8. Imagine you're Mary at the end of your life. Describe God as you, Mary, have experienced him over the years. What kind of person is he? What does he value? What has surprised you about him?

9. Fortunately, it's not up to us to decide our children's futures. But suppose you *could* choose. Which of these would you rather see your child do?

   a. Lead a safe, moral life and live to a ripe old age, raising your grandchildren to believe in Christ.

   b. Take risks in serving Christ and maybe die young in the process.

   Why would you prefer the future you chose? (If you don't like the question, tell why.)

10. What will you take with you from this discussion? Is there anything you want to do about it?

A Response of Prayer

11. Pray for the mothers in your group. You could divide into smaller groups of four to pray for specific issues. Or, one or two of you could pray for all of them together. Ask God to help each mother exult in the joy and endure the pain their children bring them. Ask him to help them raise their children to follow Mary's son, regardless of the cost.

More Mothers

The book *Daughters of Eve* also includes the stories of Eve, the first mother, and Sarah, who struggled with infertility.

NOTES
1. Luke 1:29, KJV.
2. Matthew 13:55, KJV.
3. John 2:4, KJV.
4. Mark 3:33, RSV.
5. Luke 14:26, KJV.
6. Luke 1:38, KJV.
7. John 19:26, KJV.
8. John 19:27, KJV.

2
MICHAL
Women and Marriage

1 Samuel 18:17-19:24, 25:43-44;
2 Samuel 3:1-21, 6:1-23

Michal's Story
EXCERPTED AND ADAPTED FROM *DAUGHTERS OF EVE*, PAGES 51-65.

*T*his is a story that begins like a fairy tale. The countryside is being ravaged by marauding Philistines, among whom is the giant Goliath. The king calls for a champion to fight the giant, offering the hand of his daughter as a prize to whoever defeats him. David, though the youngest of eight brothers and still a stripling, responds to the challenge and kills the giant using only a slingshot and pebbles.

The next episode continues the fairy-tale pattern. The people, overjoyed by their deliverance from the Philistines, praise this unlikely hero as he returns from battle. The women dance in the streets, inventing songs that make unpleasant comparisons between the boy David and Saul the king. Understandably jealous, the king reneges on his promise to give his oldest daughter, Merab, to David, marrying her instead to another man. David, however, does not angrily protest that she by rights belongs to him. Merab may have been too old for him anyway or simply not his type. At any rate, he humbly declares that he's just a poor sheepherder, not really fit to marry into a royal family.

Michal, however, Saul's younger daughter who is closer to

David's age, falls in love with the handsome peasant boy when her father sets him up as the court musician. When word of their romance comes to the king, he devises a way to use the young couple's attraction to his advantage. Secretly, he instructs his servants to encourage the relationship, even to suggest to David that he offer to marry Michal.

But like the younger brother in fairy tales, David is nobody's fool. For one thing, a marriage proposal included proffering a "bride-price" to the woman's family, something like a reverse dowry. David protests that he is too poor to afford the large bride-price a princess would require. But Saul is clever too. The king springs his trap: If David will bring him foreskins cut from a hundred Philistines, he will accept them as the bride-price for his daughter Michal. Of course, like any fairy-tale king, Saul believes the young hero has no hope of surviving such an assignment and only sets him the task in order to rid himself of the pesky upstart.

David, however, returns from this commission with double the number of required foreskins—from two hundred Philistine men. The king, of course, can no longer deny him without losing face. David marries Michal, who is more smitten than ever with her young lover.

David continues to lead successful raiding parties against the Philistines; the crowds love him. Even Jonathan, Saul's eldest son and heir to the throne, falls under his influence. The king grows ever more distraught by the shift in everyone's affections. Not only do his people prefer David, but his own family members are enthralled by him. Even God, it seems, has abandoned Saul for David.

After several unsuccessful attempts are made on his life in his father-in-law's court, David slips away in the night and returns to his own house where Michal is waiting for him. She tells him he won't be safe even there, though; he must flee the country altogether. Knowing that her father's spies are already watching the house, she lets her husband down on a rope from her window so that he can escape. Then she stuffs the clay body of an idol under the blanket on the bed and arranges goat hair on the pillow to look like David's. When the king's messengers demand to see her husband, she claims he is sick, giving them a peek at the decoy in the bed.

When the guards report to the king, Saul smells a rat. "I don't care how sick he is. Bring him to me, even if you have to carry him here in the bed."

When the guards return for David, Michal's subterfuge is discovered. Saul is furious. "How could you do this to me?" he shouts at her. "You're siding with my enemy."

"David told me he'd kill me if I didn't help him escape," she tells her father.

David is now a hunted man. He knows the king is likely to retaliate against his family back in Bethlehem. Therefore, he sends word for them to join him in his mountain stronghold where he is gathering a force of malcontents—mostly the poor and dispossessed in the land. His only means of supporting himself, his family, and his ragamuffin band is to provide protection for the farmers in the surrounding countryside from roving bands of raiders. In turn, the farmers supply David and his company with survival provisions.

The one person David cannot protect from the wrath of his father-in-law, however, is Michal, his young wife. She is now a virtual hostage of the king. Not only is she cut off from her husband and exposed to Saul's wrath, but her father has also lost his mind. The fairy tale isn't working out for her. In fact, it's coming apart at the seams. With her husband gone, she languishes in the power of her father the king, who soon discovers a way to punish his daughter for her disloyalty. He gives Michal away to another man. Thus he derives the dual pleasure of humbling his daughter and undermining any claims David may have to the throne by virtue of his position as Saul's son-in-law.

Michal displayed her wit when she helped David escape from her father. Yet caught in the web of court intrigue, she ends up playing the part of a pawn, powerless to affect her destiny. Michal the princess becomes Michal the slave.

Should she have been brave enough not only to engineer her husband's escape but to flee with him also? Biblical narrative, being remarkably subtle, rarely comments on the motives of its characters. Unlike, say, Aesop's fables, it does not state a bald moral at the end of the tale. Rather it usually allows the outcome of the story to speak for itself.

21

Nine years pass, while Michal lives with her new husband and David remains in exile. He marries five women in addition to Michal and has children by all of them. Michal has no children.

At length, the Philistines defeat Saul in battle and he commits suicide. Even though her father has treated her shamefully, the death of Saul comes as a blow to Michal since it strips her of whatever protection his royal status may give her. Abner, the dead king's general, has set up Michal's brother Ish-Bosheth as a puppet king over the northern part of the kingdom, though everyone knows the general pulls the strings.

In fact, Abner has little faith in Ish-Bosheth's regal abilities and sends messengers to David, inquiring what kind of deal they can make. And from this low point, Michal's star seems to rise again. The first thing David asks for as a pledge of Abner's sincerity is the return of his first wife. Her brother the puppet king is eager to grant this request and sends for his sister immediately, though as before, Michal has no voice in the matter.

And what of Phaltiel, the man who has been her husband for the past nine years? Obviously he loves his princess-bride even though she was out of favor with her father. He follows her procession along the road "weeping behind her"[1] But Abner, who cannot afford an unseemly incident in these delicate political negotiations, turns him back and tells him to go home. Phaltiel has no say in the affair either.

Was there a joyous reunion between Michal and David after all these years? Her first husband is now in his thirties, no longer an impulsive youth but a seasoned warrior and crafty politician. Has his affection for her waned as he matured and acquired a kingdom and five more wives, women who have produced plenty of offspring for him? (Michal had borne no children before David's banishment from the kingdom.) Was his request for Michal's restitution merely a political ploy, a means of cementing his monarchical claims by reaffirming his membership in Saul's family?

Again, this is one of those places where the Bible is mute about its characters' motivations. The only testimony we have are those impotent tears of her second husband, Phaltiel, and one unpleasant scene between Michal and David after her restoration.

Both as the dead king's daughter and as the new king's first wife, Michal would rule the domestic roost at the palace. Powerless for so long, used as a sexual pawn in a political game, Michal's sudden release from impotence and her elevation to first lady could not help but affect her. The other wives and their children have to answer to her now. Finally, she's in the driver's seat.

"Too long a sacrifice makes a stone of the heart," the poet Yeats wrote millennia later. And it seems possible that this is what has happened to Michal. She saved her beloved David when he was just a boy, sacrificing her marriage, her happiness, eventually her very body. She has not even had the vindication of children as Phaltiel's wife. Surrounded now by women who know her husband far better than she does, who have proved fruitful while she remains barren, her spirit turns sour, though again, Michal's inner world is presented to us only by the way she enacts it openly.

David, now ensconced in Jerusalem as king over the entire united kingdom, is eager to bring to his city the Ark of the Covenant, the central religious symbol that contains the stone tables of the commandments. To house it, he sets up before the palace a special tent, a replica of the one that had covered it during his ancestors' wanderings in the wilderness. The entrance of the Ark into the city is to be surrounded with music and great pageantry. Dancers like those who had celebrated her father's and her husband's military triumphs are to accompany the Ark. Michal's status and sex, however, preclude her participation in the festivities.

As the street crowds roar outside, Michal the queen sits in the palace at her window, looking on. Suddenly the crowd parts and she sees, not a troupe of dancing women, but her husband the king, whirling like a dervish in a most undignified way. No sense of propriety, of decorum!

Meanwhile, David is laughing and singing in the streets, dispensing gifts to the crowds like candy. She despises the sight of him leaping up and down like that—why, you can see everything! All those women hanging on him—it's disgraceful. Michal sits and fumes, impotent once more.

After the celebration, everyone having eaten and drunk his

fill and gone home, David returns to his palace to celebrate in private with his household. This has been a great day for him, a fulfillment of all those long years hiding out in the mountains, fighting and finagling to keep his ragtag band alive, holding on to hope when there seemed to be none. Finally he has united not only his people but the Lord with his people, too. But what greets him as he comes through the door brings a sudden end to his high spirits. By now Michal has worked herself into a fury. A nasty marital quarrel ensues that stirs up old hurts and grievances.

"Oh, you looked every inch a king today," she says, venom in her voice. "And the whole world could see every inch too. You looked like some kind of flasher out there. What were you doing—trying to impress the girls with your machismo?"

David is stunned. His heart, so high only moments before, plummets. He looks at this woman, the representative of the forces that hounded him and tried to deny him this triumph, and listens to her mocking him. Then his own fury erupts. "Great," he says, "just great. Well, you may think you're an expert on royal etiquette, sweetheart, but let me tell you something. It was me the Lord chose when that lousy father of yours screwed things up. It was me God wanted, not him—nor anybody from his whole lousy family. So if I want to kick up my heels and celebrate, I'm sure not going to let some has-been princess lecture me on manners. And if you were shocked by seeing a little skin today, that ain't nothing to what you're going to see."

And with that, the marriage of David and Michal was, for all intents and purposes, at an end. She lived on at the palace, still the queen, but childless, a wife in name only. As the years passed, did she take a grim pleasure in watching the tragedy that befell her erstwhile husband's household? Did the aging Michal rejoice when the lovely Bathsheba's baby, the fruit of her husband's adultery, died? And that was only the beginning.

David's other children, born to the women he accumulated in Hebron, weren't able to get along either. They later turned to incest, murder, and finally rebellion against their father the king. Did Michal feel vindicated then? We don't know. The harem was, after all, a private place, and its secrets remain undisclosed. It was, as we still say today, the children who suffered.

Your Thoughts

1. What are you feeling after reading Michal's story?

2. Can you identify with Michal in any ways? If so, how?

3. Imagine being Michal in this situation: You're newly married, and your dad wants your husband dead. Naturally, you do everything you can to help your husband escape. But would you leave home and comfort to run away and be an outlaw along with your husband, or would you stay and obey your father? Explain your reasons for your choice.

4. Put yourself in Michal's shoes again. Your husband has gone to a celebration at church and danced before God (and the whole congregation) wearing nothing but a skimpy swimsuit. Afterward, when you get him alone, your first words are:

5. What different choices do you think Michal would have made along the way if she had been following Christ and had the Holy Spirit available to her?

6. Describe a current situation in which you can choose for or against bitterness.

7. Is there anything you plan to do about what you have been discussing?

A Response of Prayer
8. Pray for each other about your answers to question 6. You might want to pair off and pray as partners. Ask God to give your partner the wisdom and other resources of the Holy Spirit to break free of bitterness in this area.

More Marriages
The book *Daughters of Eve* also tells how Ruth (a widow and non-Jew), Abigail (another of David's wives), and the Samaritan woman (who had multiple marriages) experienced marriage.

NOTE
1. 2 Samuel 3:16, KJV.

3
WOMAN WITH
THE ISSUE OF BLOOD
Women on the Outside

Mark 5:24-34, Leviticus 15:19-31

The Woman's Story
EXCERPTED AND ADAPTED FROM *DAUGHTERS OF EVE*, PAGES 88-93.

*N*othing in women's lives makes them universally feel their peculiarity so much as menstruation. Practically all cultures have some kind of ceremony to mark for girls the beginning of this monthly bleeding. These initiation ceremonies not only put the community members on notice that the girl is no longer a child but is a woman capable of bearing children, but also impress on the girl that menstruation changes her life forever in definitive, irrevocable ways.

Less technological societies often isolate menstruating women from the general community as well. Blood, especially our own, unnerves us. The bright red stain, the sensation of constant seeping, even the fetid smell of oxidizing hemoglobin assault the senses, shaming women into concealing this physical condition they find themselves in a good percentage of their lifetimes.

Women in technological societies feel a certain loss of control during menstruation, as raw nature asserts itself against our antiseptic technology. Despite the way sex education has alleviated certain fears and misunderstandings, despite frank public advertisements about "feminine hygiene products," we still don't feel the same about this physiological process as we do about, say, the buildup of dental plaque. There are women who purport to enjoy pregnancy; I have never met a woman who actually enjoys menstruating. And to bleed constantly from some inner wound for twelve years—the notion appalls us. Yet such was the condition of the woman described by the gospel writers as having "an issue of blood." [1]

Jews had regulations governing menstruating women's access to public places as well as directions about what we consider private matters—sexual relations with husbands during this period. The twelfth and fifteenth chapters of Leviticus deal specifically with these regulations, though the Jews were not unique in imposing such restrictions on women. Similar regulations limited menstruating women's access to the temples of the goddess Artemis, for example.

A woman was called "unclean" or "impure"[2] by Jewish law during her period, and though these terms were used only in a ritual context and did not necessarily connote dirtiness or sinfulness, a woman's sense of herself could not have been unaffected by the label. The rules governing menstruating women are the same as those for any community member with some sort of fluid discharge from the body (including sperm). Not only did Jewish law exclude such people from the Temple; other members of their community were not to touch them, sit in a chair they had occupied, or touch any items they might have handled. After the discharge stopped, the regulations required a ritual bath, or baptism, to prepare the person for return to activity in the community.

But what if the discharge doesn't stop? What if it goes on, day after day, week after week, even year after year? For one thing, you become anemic from constant blood loss. But that's only the physiological effect. Socially there are problems as well. Nonstop bleeding inhibits one's activities in public, makes working difficult, demands extraordinary hygienic precautions. The physical dysfunction is emotionally draining as well. The nagging sense of being out of tune with normal body cycles affects one's whole sense of self; the sufferer feels out of joint with the cosmos. And finally, there's the financial depletion from protracted medical attention.

Such was the state of the woman described in the gospels as having "an issue of blood." It's not an uncommon physical condition even today, and two thousand years of changing cultural patterns and medical progress have not altered the basic elements of her predicament. Nevertheless, she would have had to live isolated from the rest of the community during the twelve years she endured this condition. Those touching her or any of her belongings would have been considered contaminated themselves. If she were married, it would mean the end of that relationship. Friends or family could conceivably have helped her, but the constant purification ritual needed to cleanse themselves after contact with her would become a tiresome chore after a while. Though sick people were sometimes brought to Jesus by their friends or family, they usually suffered from fever or were lame or blind, not conditions that isolated the sufferer as hers did.

The Gospel of Mark provides by far the fullest account of this woman's story, though none of the versions provide her with a name. She is simply one of the nameless figures in the crowd pushing to get close to Jesus as he steps off a boat that has just brought him across the Sea of Galilee.

So famous has Jesus already become as a healer that it's all his disciples can do to keep the waiting crowds from mobbing him. A woman—an anemic one at that—didn't stand much chance in that crowd. And, in fact, someone else gets to Jesus first. An important synagogue official, someone people make way for. And, unlike the woman, he has a name—Jairus. It was probably in his own synagogue at Capernaum that a man had earlier been dispossessed of the "unclean spirit" that tormented him. At any rate, the crowd parts so that he can approach Jesus and ask him to come to his house where his twelve-year-old daughter lies near death.

The woman may have once been wealthy herself, since she has spent all her money on a variety of doctors. In fact, Mark says she has "suffered"[3] under their care, is now penniless, and all to no avail. Instead of getting better, her condition has steadily worsened. Jesus is her last hope of health. She seizes this opportunity, the lull in the crowd's clamor as Jesus stands listening to Jairus's request, to slip closer to the healer. She has no reason to believe that he would talk to her the way he's talking to Jairus. She knows she is an untouchable. The occasion calls for stealth.

We have no information as to what had convinced her that a mere touch, without even his knowledge, would be enough to heal her. Had she seen him heal others in Capernaum? Had she been friends with Peter's mother-in-law, whose fever had been chased away so easily by her son-in-law's friend? Maybe she'd heard the leper who, despite Jesus' request for anonymity, had babbled for days about the man who'd healed him. Perhaps the similarity of their positions as untouchables had first put the idea into her head. If Jesus had healed a leper and if the priest had given him a clean bill of health, maybe there was hope for her too.

At any rate, while everyone else's attention is focused on the two men who are already moving off toward Jairus' house, and knowing she will never come any closer to the healer, the woman reaches out and touches Jesus' clothes. No sooner have her fingers grazed the fabric than she feels the blood cease to flow from her body.

Jesus stops in the middle of the road, people jamming up against him. "Who did that?" he demands, looking around. "Who touched me?"[4]

His companions shake their heads. "What do you mean?" they ask impatiently. "Here we are, about to be trampled by this mob, and you want to know who touched you?" Neither they nor we understand the mechanics of how this healing power works. Just as the woman immediately feels in her body that she is healed, so Jesus knows in himself that power has gone out of him. From his disciples' remark it's clear other people were jostling him, very possibly wanting some miracle themselves. But only this woman's touch called forth Jesus' healing power.

The woman is understandably afraid. She knows this man has every right to be angry since she has defiled him. Expecting a rebuke, she falls down before him, confessing what she has done as if it were a crime, expecting his anger.

Instead, his response is unexpectedly gentle. His first word to her is "Daughter."[5] This, to one to whom every human contact has, for twelve long years, been denied. The very word must be like balm to her terror, implying as it does not merely connection but protection. In one word Jesus reassures her that her infraction of the regulations will bring her no harm. At the same time, however, he doesn't patronize her by saying, "I know you're a poor, sick woman, desperate enough to try anything. And I'm overlooking this incident, but next time, make an appointment." (One of the most appealing characteristics of Jesus is the way he dealt with individuals immediately. He never had scheduling problems or an appointment calendar.)

Instead, he applauds rather than condemns her audacity: "It's your faith that's healed you," he tells her. If she hadn't been willing to relinquish what little dignity she had left, she might never have been whole again. If she hadn't put aside her fear of embarrassment and exposure, she could not receive the peace he now bestows on her as a blessing. That's why this woman's touch is different from the others'. Undoubtedly many in the crowd wanted to be healed, but she was the one who had something at risk.

Living faith—the kind that calls forth a response—stakes its life on the answer. When we approach God, however hesitantly, we are always teetering on the margin of life whether we recognize it or not. Faith never comes alive except on the edge. Hedging one's bets is not the same as having faith. An instructive contrast to this woman is Nicodemus, a wealthy, well-educated man who, despite his protected position, nevertheless comes to Jesus by night rather than in the press of the crowd. What he wanted from Jesus was philosophical discussion. Perhaps Jesus' use of a physiological metaphor—being born again—was chosen in order to show Nicodemus how much was at stake, that faith is a life-and-death matter.

The lap of luxury stifles faith; the life of emotional comfort smothers it. That's why it's always the marginal people Jesus notices. Not only this woman but the widow who put her two pennies—all she had—into the temple treasury. If the woman with the issue of blood had not yet spent all her money on doctors, she might still have clung to the hope that they could cure her. The end of our rope is where we're always closest to God.

Your Thoughts
1. What fresh insights into this story did you gain from the above account?

2. What message did you get as a young woman from parents, men, or others regarding menstruation? Did you ever feel "unclean"? (If you feel comfortable doing so, tell a story about one of your earliest experiences of menstruation.)

3. a. Can you identify in any ways with this woman who was suffering for so long? Explain.

   b. In what ways has your experience with suffering been different from this woman's?

   c. This woman's suffering propelled her into an encounter with Jesus. How has your experience with suffering (or perhaps the lack of it) affected your faith in Jesus?

4. How would you describe Jesus in this story? What character or values do you see him display?

5. Are you more like the people who waited politely in the crowd, hoping for a dignified encounter with Jesus? Or are you more like this desperate woman, who rushed in with little thought of dignity?

6. a. What was this woman risking by acting with faith? What did she have to lose?

   b. Have you ever had to take a risk in order to receive something from God? If so, tell about that experience.

   c. Are you currently facing any faith risk? What might you lose if you take this risk? What might you gain?

7. Let's say you have a need for healing. What risks are involved in praying aloud for yourself about this need in front of the other women in your group? What might you have to lose?

A Response of Prayer

8. a. Take a moment of silence to ask yourself, "What healing or other intervention do I need from Jesus?" Then ask yourself, "Is it worth the risk to pray about this in front of this group?"

   b. After a minute of silence, let the group leader begin your time of prayer by asking for one thing for herself. Then allow time for others to express their own requests for themselves. No one should feel obligated to say something aloud.

More Marginalized Women

The book *Daughters of Eve* also tells about Hagar the slave and the Syro-Phoenician woman, a mother from a race despised by Jews.

NOTES

1. Mark 5:25, KJV.
2. Leviticus 15:25, NIV.
3. Mark 5:26, KJV.
4. Luke 8:45, NIV.
5. Mark 5:34, KJV.

4
MARTHA
Single Women

Luke 10:38-42, John 11:1-46

Martha's Story

EXCERPTED AND ADAPTED FROM *DAUGHTERS OF EVE*, PAGES 96-105.

*L*uke gives us our earliest view of Martha of Bethany. In a deceptively simple domestic scene, one that sets the tone for the later episodes, we see Martha preparing a meal in her home. We don't know if she knew Jesus before he decided to stop over at her house in a suburb of Jerusalem, or if he merely showed up in Bethany and waited for someone to invite him to supper. Earlier in the same chapter Jesus had directed seventy-two of his followers to go ahead of him into all the towns he expected to visit, instructing them to take no provisions but instead to depend on the hospitality they encountered there. However poor such accommodations might prove, the disciples were not to criticize but to eat what was set before them.

So perhaps this advance team had already made arrangements with Martha for Jesus' arrival—along with his twelve disciples, an important detail in the story that is often overlooked. No wonder Martha is nervous about dinner preparations; she'll have at least thirteen guests at her table tonight.

And it *is* her table. Though she has a sister, Mary, and a brother, Lazarus, the story emphasizes that the house belongs to Martha. There's a possibility that she was a widow, but Luke, who frequently uses that term to identify other women in his narrative, does not classify Martha as one. Nor is she called "the wife of" or even "the daughter of," the ancient world's way of providing women with a last name. In this first encounter with Jesus, even Lazarus, the brother of these women, is not mentioned, possibly an indication he is a good bit younger than the two sisters. Thus the strongest probability is that Martha was a single woman, as was her sister Mary.

As to Martha's social position, it's hard to know how much to make of the fact that Martha's name means "lady," the feminine form of "lord" in Hebrew. Nevertheless, whether because of inheritance or her own business acumen, Martha is well enough off to own her own home. And socially sensitive enough to be concerned about hosting such a notable guest as Jesus. On the other hand, she is not so wealthy that she can simply leave all the dinner preparations to servants. Indeed, this fact occasions the conflict in the story. While Martha is bustling about in the kitchen, her sister Mary is ignoring her responsibilities and sitting in the living room, absorbed in the "man-talk" of Jesus and his followers.

Sweating over a hot stove in the kitchen while others are enjoying themselves is guaranteed to put anyone out of sorts. "Distracted"[1] is the way the *New International Version* describes Martha's mental and emotional state. The *King James Version* says she was "cumbered."[2] The Greek verb only occurs this once in the New Testament and means literally "to draw around." Martha has drawn around her like a barricade the complications that automatically attend a large dinner party. Paradoxically, this screens her off as well from the *pièce de résistance* of the evening, Jesus himself. Finally, flushed and frustrated with too much to do and too little help, Martha flounces into the living room and makes a scene, complaining to the very guest she is purposing to honor about her sister's behavior.

Which is precisely what she needed to do.

Martha's social *faux pas*, her plaintive wail, cracks the otherwise smooth surface of the evening, and out of that crack comes boiling the volcanic truth of Martha's soul—resentment and a feeling of abandonment. "Lord, don't you care?" she cries. "Mary's not helping at all. I'm having to do all the work by myself. Tell her she has to help me." The words burst from her with the injured tone of a child protesting cosmic injustice. *It isn't fair! It isn't fair!*

Every woman in the world has felt like Martha. (Which is why countless Sunday school classes and women's circles are named after her.) And not just while slaving over a hot stove listening to other people laughing and talking in the living room. There's also being left alone with the laundry while everyone else goes off to work or to class where work is recognized and appreciated. At home, no one rewards you with money or grades for the drudgery you do. You clock long years of child rearing, and later, of being tied down by aging or sick parents—all the jobs that have to be done but never get noticed. Jobs everyone else in the world seems to avoid successfully—except you.

It's bad enough that husbands, sons, fathers, brothers manage to opt out of those responsibilities—but another woman? Your own sister? Who does she think she is, anyway? Thus is Martha—thus are we all—reduced to childish, impotent rage at the overwhelming inequity of our unacknowledged lives spent in unappreciated labor. Doesn't anybody care?

Martha's indignation is honest, straight from the bottom of her soul, and that is why it was right. Much better to say straight out to Jesus what's on your mind than to take the more devious approach, the one that says, "Oh no. Never mind. I'm fine. Go ahead and have a good time. Don't worry about me."

Throughout the gospels Jesus constantly asks people, "What do you want?" or "What do you want me to do for you?" And as long as people tell him frankly the desire of their heart, they get it. In Martha's situation, however, Jesus can't give her precisely what she asks for without taking it away from someone else, in this case, her sister. Nevertheless, he hears the deepest stratum of her bitterness: "Don't you care?" *Don't I matter too?*

And in this complex narrative, compressed into a mere five sentences, Luke expends two words to have Jesus repeat her name as a prelude to his response—"Martha, Martha."[3] Though Luke wastes no adjectives describing his tone of voice, in the very repetition of her name we hear the nuances. Since she has spoken as a child, Jesus calms the child in her. Simultaneously, however, the very naming affirms her significance. To him she is not an unimportant kitchen flunky but an individual.

But we also catch a tone of regret, even see him shake his head slightly. He will not grant the more overt part of her request—that he order her sister into the kitchen also. Misery may love company, but one injustice cannot be assuaged by inflicting another. Instead, he describes to Martha her current condition: "You're upset and distracted by details." Then he tells her the hard truth: "But only one thing is actually necessary. Mary has chosen that. And it won't be taken from her."

There's much to be unpacked from this response. Note, for one thing, that Martha's distraction really is with the superfluities of social life, not inescapably essential domestic chores. Jesus doesn't trivialize domestic duties by brushing them aside as insignificant. Martha, after all, is not changing diapers or doing the weekly laundry.

The two sisters have been given what both must have seen as a remarkable opportunity—having this great teacher as a guest in their home. How they decide to take advantage of that opportunity is their own choice. Do they spend the time putting on a big spread or do they use it listening to what he has to say? A man who's just sent seventy-two people out into the countryside with only the cloaks on their backs is hardly going to encourage his other supporters to dither over social superfluities. He's only moving his Sermon on the Mount indoors here, telling Martha to consider the lilies of the field. Anxiety about what to eat or drink is a problem for women as well as men—maybe more so. But it's a predicament he's offering to free Martha from.

The trick, however, is that the freedom has to be chosen. One has to deliberately embrace the one necessary thing instead of the many distracting things. Mary, he says, *chose* the better part. It was not a part assigned to her by her culture, certainly. Her very presence there in the living room among the male disciples no doubt occasioned a few raised eyebrows. Nevertheless, having chosen, she cannot have it taken away. Not to placate public perceptions of what is seemly; not even to assuage the private feelings of her sister.

It is interesting that Luke tells this story from Martha's point of view. Mary never speaks or acts in the whole scene. Was she aware of her sister's distress? Was she embarrassed by her outburst? We don't know. Just as we don't know how Martha responded to Jesus.

We do know, however, that the friendship between the great man and the two women of Bethany continued, because they reappear in his story some time later at what was a critical point in all their lives. The Jerusalem religious establishment has sought to end increasingly bitter controversies by attempting to take Jesus into custody. Jesus then retreats from Judea to the far side of the Jordan, the site of his baptism where his ministry began. Even there, however, he continues to draw large crowds.

While there he receives word from the two sisters that their brother Lazarus is sick. It is a simple message, emphasizing the bond between the two men; it does not request that Jesus leave his safe haven to come and heal their brother. Though they no doubt wish this were possible, the two women refrain from making the request explicit since they know a return to Bethany—less than two miles from Jerusalem—would expose Jesus to grave danger, a fact that's often been overlooked in dealing with this story.

And indeed, Jesus makes no move to return. His remark— "This sickness is not unto death"[4]—the disciples no doubt took at the time to mean that Lazarus' illness would not prove fatal. But lest we think his remark unfeeling, the gospel repeats for emphasis the fact that Jesus "loved Martha, and her sister, and Lazarus,"[5] again naming Martha first as though she is the acknowledged head of the household.

Finally, after two days, Jesus announces to his disciples that they're heading back to Judea. His companions are aghast. "You're going back? But they just tried to stone you there!" Jesus, however, is determined, and subtly reminds them of their own obligation to the Bethany family by calling Lazarus "*our* friend"[6] whom he knows has already died. As Jesus and his band near Bethany, they hear that Lazarus was indeed buried four days ago.

Meanwhile, Jews from Jerusalem have come to Bethany to join Martha and Mary in the customary Jewish mourning ceremonies, which last for a full week. When Martha hears that Jesus is coming, she slips out of the house and goes to intercept him, leaving the guests to Mary this time—the guests who surely pose a threat to her friend. Her emotions are mixed, to say the least, when she sees him. While fearing for his safety, she's also still grieving for her brother, so a slight reproach colors her greeting to Jesus: "This wouldn't have happened if you had been here." Then she adds, with a surge of hope, "But you can still fix it. God always listens to you and does what you ask."

Jesus replies matter-of-factly, "Your brother will rise again."[7]

No doubt Martha, always conventional herself, hears this as one of those rote phrases by which we offer one another condolences. As if reciting a catechism, she parrots back to him the accepted Jewish belief in a general resurrection at the end of time. But we can hear the disappointment in her voice. A catechism is cold comfort at this moment, though it looks as if that's all she's likely to get from Jesus.

"No," he says. "You don't understand. *I* am the resurrection and the life. If you believe that, it doesn't matter if he's dead. He'll live again."

"Okay, okay," she replies. She's never been particularly interested in theological discussions and certainly doesn't have time for one now. "I know. You're the Messiah, the one we've been waiting for to come into the world." Within, however, she's probably thinking, *But what good has that done me? My brother's dead now. I don't want to have to wait till the end of time to see him again.*

Then she hurries away, leaving him there in the graveyard, and goes home to get her sister who will no doubt get more out of all this religious talk than she has.

Back at the house, she must be cautious because the Jerusalem Jews are still there. She tells Mary secretly about Jesus' arrival, adding—a kind touch—that the rabbi is calling for her in particular.

Overcome by excitement, Mary recklessly rushes out of the house and up the road to the cemetery. When Mary sees Jesus she falls at his feet. She may have more of an intellectual bent than her older sister, but her feelings at the moment mirror Martha's; thus her first words are similar. "If you had been here, this would never have happened. Lazarus wouldn't have died." Like her sister, she has enough faith to believe Jesus can stave off death by healing people. But bring them back to life again? All well-informed Jews knew the soul only lingers in the vicinity of the body for three days, during which a healer might manage a miraculous restoration. But after four days, all hope has to be abandoned.

Mary has been so reckless in running from the house to see Jesus, however, that the entire mourning party has noticed and followed her. Before the two friends know it they are surrounded by suspicious Jerusalemites. Jesus looks around distressed. The word used here to describe his reaction has been variously translated as "groaned inwardly," "was deeply moved," and "was angry." Except for this story, the Greek verb is used nowhere else in the New Testament, though the Greek playwright Aeschylus employed it to describe the snorting of horses. Certainly, the word betokens intense emotional expression and is coupled in the sentence with "troubled." Does it mean Jesus was distressed at his friends' lack of faith or understanding? Was he upset by the sudden appearance of his enemies? Or was he overwhelmed by his own sorrow at Lazarus' death?

He raises his voice over the wails of the mourners and merely asks, "Where have you buried him?" When they point out the tomb, a limestone cave sealed up with a stone in the same fashion his own would shortly be, Jesus begins to weep as well.

This time the gospel puts our questions about the specific reason for this display of emotion into the mouths of the bystanders. Some believe he is mourning for his well-loved friend; others think these are tears of self-reproach for not having come soon enough to heal Lazarus of the fatal illness. Instead of confirming either of these speculations, the gospel once more says that Jesus "snorted." "Remove the stone," he commands.[8]

Martha, practical to the point of bluntness, protests: "But he'll stink by now!"

"Didn't I tell you that if you'd believe you'd see God's glory?" Jesus asks.

By now the others have wrestled the stone from the entrance to the cave. The people crowding around are holding their collective breath. But Jesus pauses, then begins to speak, addressing his words skyward: "Father, I give you thanks for hearing me. I know you always hear me, but I'm saying this aloud for the sake of those standing around here so that they can believe that you've sent me." No doubt he particularly had Martha in mind. Jesus has known since he received word of Lazarus' illness on the far side of the Jordan four days and many miles ago that he would restore his friend to life, give him back to his sisters. What distresses Jesus is the unnecessary heartache these friends, the ones who know him best, still insist on inflicting on themselves. It all seems so simple to him. Yet no amount of teaching seems to penetrate their understanding. Whether it's dinner or death makes little difference; they're always bothered about the wrong thing.

Jesus takes a deep breath. "Lazarus," he cries. "Come out!"

And out of the mouth of the cave shuffles the startling figure of Lazarus, still wrapped mummylike in strips of linen burial bandages. The sight had to be at once astonishing and appalling, like a scene from a horror movie. Everyone is so immobilized, both with hope and with dread of walking corpses, that Jesus has to tell them to unwind the bandages and free Lazarus.

In her jubilation over her brother's restoration, Martha decides to throw another dinner party. The gospel once again puts Martha in the kitchen, just as she was before, slaving over the hot stove. This time, however, without protest. Perhaps because she's so filled with gratitude that she needs the outlet of physical activity to express it. But also she now sees that this is work, not imposed, but freely chosen. Her own last supper with her Lord is her gift, not her duty.

In Catholic and Orthodox traditions, the sisters Martha and Mary have been emblematic of the two different spiritual paths. Martha is the active "server." That Greek verb—from which our word "deacon" derives—is always attached to her in the Bible. Martha expresses her devotion through physical action. Too often, however, her service has been interpreted as that of someone who hovers in the background, patient and practically invisible. But when we look at her story, we find that Martha's serving does not make her less assertive. She speaks up, forges ahead, takes charge. As head of her household, she doesn't hesitate to cause a scene at a dinner party. She's the one who hurries out to intercept Jesus when he returns to Bethany and who tries to keep his presence secret from his enemies. She even argues with Jesus about opening her brother's tomb. Martha is not a follower, but a leader.

Whether active or contemplative, both these women had to be single for this story to happen, given the cultural climate of the times. Only as head of her household would Martha have had the effrontery to burst into the living room with her complaint. Not she but her husband would have gone out to meet Jesus at her brother's tomb. Married, Mary would not have sat at Jesus' feet but only heard his words secondhand.

Women with husbands and children cannot reasonably expect to fulfill the duties that come with the life they've chosen and also throw themselves wholeheartedly into a cause or work night and day. When marriage fuses the very flesh of two people, it merges their time and energy as well. Schedules have to be coordinated, work organized, behavior moderated. All action is undertaken knowing it affects another person.

Martha could both serve and speak up precisely because she was single. There are some freedoms only bestowed on the single state.

Your Thoughts

1. How would you describe Martha? What kind of person is she? What is important to her?

2. In what ways are you like Martha? In what ways are you different?

3. Describe Jesus in these scenes. What kind of person is he? What does he value?

4. What do you admire about Martha?

5. Have you ever felt "rage at the overwhelming inequity of our unacknowledged lives spent in unappreciated labor"? If so, tell about that feeling.

6. How do you generally deal with rage toward Jesus (as Martha felt at the dinner) or with doubt of him (as she felt when her brother died)? Do you generally express feelings like these to Jesus, or do you push them down or hold them in? Why do you suppose you do that?

7. Do you think Martha is missing something because she doesn't have a husband? Explain.

8. Does this discussion prompt you to any action?

A Response of Prayer

9. Pray for the single women in your group. Express appreciation for ways in which they have served you. Ask God to give them opportunities to exercise their gifts.

More Single Women

The book *Daughters of Eve* also includes the stories of Jephthah's daughter and Mary Magdalene.

NOTES

1. Luke 10:40, NIV.
2. Luke 10:40, KJV.
3. Luke 10:41, KJV.
4. John 11:4, KJV.
5. John 11:5, KJV.
6. John 11:11, KJV.
7. John 11:23, NIV.
8. John 11:39, NASB.

5
RIZPAH
Women and Violence

2 Samuel 3:6-11, 21:1-14

Rizpah's Story
EXCERPTED AND ADAPTED FROM *DAUGHTERS OF EVE*, PAGES 117-121.

*M*aybe she was a raving beauty whose good looks were the catalyst for a disaster. Maybe she was simply being used as a pawn in a power play by an ambitious military man. Whatever the unrecorded particulars of the case, Rizpah's private tragedy is buried at the heart of a larger tale of intrigue and political maneuvering—and not without purpose.

After Israel's first king, Saul, and his son Jonathan were killed in battle, the country passed into the hands of Saul's second and much weaker son, Ish-Bosheth. The real power behind the throne, however, was Abner, the general who had led Saul's army. Whether as a means of solidifying his position as quasi king or because he had cast his eye on Saul's concubine for some time, no sooner was the old king dead than Abner claimed Rizpah for himself. Ish-Bosheth objected to the general taking such liberties with his dead father's concubine. It showed flagrant disrespect for Saul's memory, he said. (If anyone consulted Rizpah herself on the matter, it is not recorded.)

Abner exploded. "You have me to thank for saving you from David's army. And all you can do is criticize me for taking what should have been given to me as a reward!" Ish-Bosheth, quaking in his royal sandals, was too intimidated by the general to respond.

This further demonstration of his king's weakness must have pushed Abner over the edge. At any rate, he seized the occasion to change sides in Israel's six-year struggle with David's rebel forces. After conferring in secret with the elders of Israel, he set out with a delegation to Hebron, David's stronghold, and cut a deal with him. Abner hadn't reckoned, however, with the jealousy of David's own general, Joab. Before Abner could return to Jerusalem, Joab lured him into an ambush and murdered him.

How did this conspiracy affect Rizpah's fortunes back in Jerusalem? We're not told. With Abner dead, she would have little protection during the siege of the city that followed. Ish-Bosheth cannot protect her since he himself is killed by a couple of his own mercenaries, who decided to throw in their lot with David. However, since David, ever faithful to his old master Saul, had Ish-Bosheth's murderers hung and their mutilated bodies publicly displayed as a warning to those who would harm any of Saul's offspring, it's possible that Rizpah's connection to Saul ensured her protection and maintenance.

At any rate, she was still around several years later when David, now firmly established in the unified kingdom, has to deal with a three-year famine brought on by drought. When he inquires of the Lord as to the famine's cause, he is told that Saul left behind a piece of unfinished business. It seems that at some point in his reign, during the height of his military exploits, he had promised to spare a group called the Gibeonites from slaughter. Obviously, Saul must have reneged on his promise—though the details of this battle are not recorded in the Bible—because now the Gibeonites are seeking restitution, and the Lord is taking their side by withholding rain from Israel until the matter is cleared up. David offers to make a cash settlement, but the Gibeonites refuse to accept anything but the hardest of currencies—blood. The blood of Saul's heirs. Seven of them.

David himself is now caught between vows. Having promised Jonathan that he would look after his children, David cannot hand over his friend's son Mephibosheth to the Gibeonites. So he gives them instead the five sons of Saul's daughter Merab. Plus Saul's only surviving sons, the children of the concubine Rizpah.

One fine spring morning, the seven are impaled by the Gibeonites on a mountaintop near Saul's hometown. The bodies are to be left there, exposed all summer long till the time when the autumn rains should begin, which will signal the end of the drought and famine.

Now, for the first time, Rizpah enters the story as something more than a sexual pawn in political maneuvering. She takes action—the only action possible for a woman in her shaky position. Certainly neither she nor Merab could protect their sons from death. But after enduring that inevitability, Rizpah still performs the only meaningful deed open to her. Carrying sackcloth up to the mountain where the sacrificial victims have been left exposed to the elements, she spreads it over the bodies. Then she camps out there all summer long. During the day she beats off the vultures that would otherwise peck out the eyes and entrails of the corpses. At night she fends off the jackals that would strip the flesh from the skeletons and scatter the bones.

At this point, Rizpah's macabre vigil reminds me of Antigone's from Greek tragedy. In Sophocles' play, the daughter of the deposed king Oedipus opposes her uncle Creon by symbolically honoring the corpse of her slain brother who had been left to lie exposed to the sun and vultures as a warning to other rebels. And certainly both of these stories show how ancient cultures set great store on honoring the dead by not allowing desecration of the body. Antigone's defiance earned her own death and her country more suffering, while Rizpah's humble efforts proved to be the hinge that turned events toward renewed health for the land.

Word of how Rizpah was defending the dead bodies from desecration eventually made its way to David's ear. No doubt feeling reproached by her pitiful devotion, the king followed her example. He has the bones of Saul and Jonathan retrieved from Jabesh-gilead and buried in the family sepulcher—along with the sacrificed remains of Saul's sons and grandsons.

And interestingly, it was *then*, rather than after the sacrificial slaughter of Saul's progeny, that God answered the prayers for an end to the famine. Was it mercy he desired all along, and not sacrifice? Go back and read the story closely and you'll see that, when

David finally consulted the Lord after three years of famine, he was told merely that the present hard times were the result of Saul and his blood-crazed heirs killing the Gibeonites off in a frenzy of "ethnic cleansing." He was given no instructions as to how to amend the situation. Never did the Lord order David to accede to the Gibeonites' wishes for human sacrifice. Nor, for that matter, did David ask.

It was only later, after he heard of Rizpah's pitifully desperate measures, that it occurred to him to follow suit and give his old enemy Saul and his heirs a "decent burial." And because of that long-delayed display of mercy, the land was healed.

Rizpah's story also reminds me of a contemporary woman, Yvonne Bezejah, a Brazilian socialite, whose life of privilege was dramatically challenged one night when she witnessed the slaughter of six "street kids" in the Candeleria district of Rio de Janeiro. The city's thieves often recruit abandoned children to steal for them, creating a crime problem for the Rio police. On that night alone, the extermination squad had rounded up and killed sixty children in different parts of the city. Across the street from Rio's largest church, Yvonne stood watch all night over the bodies of six children to keep the police from disposing of the bodies. A lone woman, she could not stop the slaughter, but her vigil exposed to the world the hideous truth beneath Rio's veneer of wealth and glamor.

Looking back from our vantage point of three millennia, it is easy to find plenty to object to in Rizpah's story. The practice of concubinage itself. Abner's demonstrating his power by claiming rights to her sexual use. Her sons publicly butchered. But we are all circumscribed in one way or another by the age in which we live. Cultural strictures often keep us from both seeing and acting upon opportunities to show mercy. We do more honor to Rizpah and her womanhood by focusing instead on how she made the most of her one small opportunity. She wasn't given a lot of latitude, either by her culture or her circumstances. After everything had been taken away from her—her youth, her beauty, her male protectors—she took what she still had—her mother's grief—and acted upon it. And taught a lesson to Israel's greatest king that saved his nation.

Your Thoughts

1. How do you respond emotionally to Rizpah's story?

2. If you had lived Rizpah's life, what do you think you would believe about God?

3. a. In Acts 13:22, the Apostle Paul calls King David "a man after God's heart." What impression do you get of this "man after God's heart" from Rizpah's story?

   b. Are you surprised that Paul could speak so highly of David? Explain.

4. a. What do you think would have happened if Rizpah had gone to David and protested the killing of her sons?

b. A shrewd but indirect tactic is often more effective than a frontal assault, especially when we lack power, as Rizpah did. What was shrewd about the way Rizpah handled her sons' deaths?

c. What risk was Rizpah taking by standing guard over her sons' bodies?

5. What do you think you would do if your government sacrificed your children? (Such a thing is not uncommon in our world.)

6. Rizpah was the victim of repeated violence to her own body and her family. What do you like or not like about the way she responded to being a victim?

7. Have you ever suffered violence? If so, how have you responded?

8. What opportunities do you have to act for justice?

A Response of Prayer
9. Pray for women you know (including those in your group) who have suffered violence upon themselves or their loved ones. Pray for healing and for shrewd opportunities to use these evil circumstances for redemptive purposes.

More Women and Violence
The book *Daughters of Eve* also includes the stories of the rape of Tamar and a woman caught in adultery.

6
MARY OF BETHANY
Sensual Women

Luke 10:38-42; John 11:1-46, 12:1-8
[Matthew 26:6-13; Mark 14:1-11]

Mary's Story
EXCERPTED AND ADAPTED FROM *DAUGHTERS OF EVE*, PAGES 143-146.

*D*espite the fact that Mary of Bethany's complete story must be pieced together from bits of all four gospels, it maintains an inner consistency that reveals this woman's peculiar qualities. Unlike her sister Martha, whom we have already seen as an active, practical person, Mary is quiet and introspective. Not the sort we would ordinarily call sensual. But there is more to Mary than first meets the eye. Though ordinarily she stays in the background, she is drawn irresistibly toward the man Jesus with an intensity found in no other person in the gospels.

In Luke's story about the two sisters, Mary never speaks, not even to defend herself from her sister's implicit charge of laziness. Her only act is in choosing. Otherwise she was passive. She sits at Jesus' feet and listens to his words. When her sister bustles in to point her accusing finger, Mary remains silent, allowing Jesus to speak for her.

The "good part," Jesus calls Mary's choice, "which shall not be taken away from her."[1] And we still have a hard time accepting that judgment. In order to protect that choice of Mary's, the Roman Catholic Church institutionalized the quiet stillness called contemplation, distinguishing it from more active orders of religion who busy themselves with good works. In the Protestant tradition, Mary's choice has an even harder time gaining acceptance, much less respect. Cultivation of the inner life, which requires sitting and listening, looks like loafing to us whose work ethic often becomes a works theology. Yet this is not the only time Jesus defends Mary's choice.

The impractical, impulsive side of her nature shows again when her brother Lazarus dies and the mourning party from Jerusalem arrives at the sisters' home. Martha, hearing that Jesus is approaching, slips out of the house to warn him that potential enemies are there. But Mary thoughtlessly rushes out of the house to meet him, not stopping to consider the consequences for her Lord.

As it turns out, however, not all of the Jerusalem Jews who witness the raising of Lazarus react negatively. This unmistakable sign of Jesus' divine power, in fact, convinces some of them that he is the Messiah. Mary's impetuous rush to see Jesus was the catalyst that eventually brought them to belief.

Others who witness the miracle, however, hurry back to the religious officials in Jerusalem and report that this man is a worse threat than they had heretofore imagined. The marvel in Bethany sets in motion the plans to arrest Jesus.

Matthew and Mark both place the next Bethany scene at the home of someone called Simon the Leper, while John locates it at the sisters' home. Was Lazarus, like Peter, also called Simon? Had his death in fact been caused by leprosy, a disease that would require him to live outside the city, thus leaving the house in Martha's hands? Now that he was healed and could live at home again, did Matthew and Mark designate the house as his? Whatever the answer to those questions, it is obvious that neither of those two gospel writers was as familiar with the Bethany family as John. As if to clarify Matthew and Mark's account, John emphasizes that the Mary present at the raising of Lazarus is the same woman who plays a central role in this following scene.

Since Jesus intends to celebrate the Passover this year in Jerusalem, he decides to spend the next week at Martha's house in Bethany, only a few miles from the city. Martha is in the kitchen again, preparing a dinner both to honor her guest and celebrate her brother's restoration. And Mary has once more left her sister to do the work.

But this time she goes to unpack a secret treasure she's squirreled away for some special occasion—an entire pint of an expensive perfume. (Mark prices the contents of the alabaster container at three hundred denarii, almost a year's wages for a working man.) She slips into the dining room where the guests are reclining, assembled to celebrate her brother's new life. Approaching the couch where Jesus reclines, without a word of explanation she opens the vessel and pours it—all of it—over Jesus' feet. As the heavy scent rises, filling the room, the other people turn to stare. Then slowly, deliberately, she takes down her long hair and begins to wipe the feet of the man she loves above all others.

Throughout the entire scene, Mary never speaks. In fact, the only time Mary ever speaks is to echo her sister's words at her brother's tomb. Whereas Martha is never at a loss for words, Mary appears reticent in the extreme. She is forced to find other ways to express her devotion.

But Mary is proclaiming something more than simple emotion by this act. Her bizarre exhibition of love is much like the symbolic acts used by earlier Hebrew prophets to deliver their messages. Jeremiah used a rotten linen belt to illustrate his nation's decay; Mary is using her perfume to prophesy what lies ahead for Jesus. She sees what the others do not. Not much more than a week ago her brother came shuffling out of his tomb, grave clothes flapping around him. Another week and there will be another body, another tomb. She alone among Jesus' followers takes to heart his warnings about his approaching death.

Like most prophets, however, Mary and her message go unheeded. The other guests see only a woman with loose hair— something they understand easily enough. In fact, the disciples are outraged by Mary's behavior, finding it immodest, shocking— as well as an extravagant waste of the perfume.

"Shameful," they mutter amongst themselves. Judas, the treasurer of the group, speaks what they're all thinking. "We could have done a lot of good with that. If she didn't need it, she could have given it to us. We'd have seen to it that the poor benefited from it at least."

Jesus, unperturbed by her act, speaks up immediately. "Just a minute here," he says. "Leave her alone. Don't you understand what this act of hers signifies? I'm going to die. And she's the only one who sees that. That's why she's used the perfume this way—to prepare me for burial." Then he points out the same thing to them he told Martha when she complained against her sister earlier. "There's nothing to stop you from doing what you want to. It's your choice. You can give to the poor anytime you want to. They're always there, ready and waiting for your charity. Me, on the other hand, you may not have around much longer."

Matthew extends Jesus' defense of Mary: "What she's done for me here is beautiful. Wherever my story is told she'll be a part of it. She'll never be forgotten." And indeed, Mary's story appears in all four gospels.

Mary remains in the background, except when her passion overwhelms her passivity. Her only means of expressing her inward ardor is aesthetic and symbolic. We *hear* Martha; we *see* Mary, her face veiled by her long hair as she wipes the perfume she's spilled on her Lord's feet. She *enacts* love; our memories are marked with the sight.

Jesus never upbraids anyone in the gospels for extravagance. In fact, he applauds it. He's all for generosity, never a utilitarian. In our culture, we tend to side with Judas. "She has done something beautiful for me," Jesus said. But what use is beauty? You can't eat it. It doesn't pay the bills. Yet it points beyond itself, in the direction of all our hungers.

When we grasp at beauty and try to possess it for ourselves, we become like Potiphar's wife, prisoners of sensuality. But when we allow our senses to aim us toward the source of beauty itself, we become like Mary—lavish with love.

Your Response

1. What do you like about Mary of Bethany? Is there anything you don't like?

2. a. If you had a wise spiritual teacher and his friends over to your house for dinner, would you be more likely to be sitting in the living room with the guests or bustling in the kitchen?

b. Why do you suppose you're like that?

3. How easy is it for you to spend intimate time with Jesus? What kinds of things make it easy or hard for you?

4. What would happen if you carved out a full hour each week to be alone with Jesus?

5. Mary's demonstration of worship toward Jesus was extremely sensual. How do you demonstrate worship toward him? Do you tend to be sensual in your worship or more restrained?

6. Do you think of yourself as a sensual person? Explain.

A Response of Prayer

7. Spend some time silently worshiping God, alone or with your group. Close your eyes and just be with him, as though you were Mary sitting at Jesus' feet. If your group is unaccustomed to being silent together, you could plan just one or two minutes of silence.

   To begin your period of silence, one person could read aloud John 12:1-8 while the others close their eyes and focus on worshiping Jesus for his goodness, beauty, and power over death.

More Sensual Women

The book *Daughters of Eve* also includes the stories of Potiphar's wife and the Shulamite maiden in the Song of Songs.

NOTE
1. Luke 10:42, NIV.

7
REBEKAH
Manipulative Women

Genesis 24:1-67, 25:19-34,
26:1-11, 27:1-46

Rebekah's Story
EXCERPTED AND ADAPTED FROM *DAUGHTERS OF EVE*, PAGES 149-158.

*T*he shadow of Sarah, Abraham's wife and the first Hebrew
matriarch, falls across the story of Rebekah, the daughter-
in-law she never knew. This strong-willed woman, who had conspired with her husband against pharaohs and kings, who had the
audacity to laugh at angels, continued to exert her influence over
her son Isaac even after her death. When he was still a child, she
had been so jealous for his prerogatives, so fearful that Hagar's
older boy might supplant him, that she had driven the slave
woman and her child into the desert to die. Sarah had been fierce
in her protection of Isaac; it was his father who had actually taken
him up on Mount Moriah with the intention of making him a
human sacrifice. Small wonder then that Isaac, still mourning his
mother's death, remained unmarried at forty.

Sarah was already in her grave by the time Abraham sent his
trusted steward back to northern Syria to find a wife for his son
among his own people. Abraham, himself 140 years old, knew he
might not survive till the steward returned from the long journey
back to Padan-Aram on the far side of the Euphrates River.

"What if I can't find a woman willing to leave her family to
come to this faroff land?" the steward asks, scrupulously trying

to anticipate every contingency. He also realizes Abraham could die before his return.

"Whatever happens, don't let Isaac go back to my homeland. Canaan is the land that's been promised to us. He has to stay here, even if you can't find him a wife there," Abraham tells him.

Isaac himself is never consulted about these arrangements. Abraham gives the steward complete power over his son's destiny. And indeed, Isaac plays an exceptionally passive role throughout his lifetime.

When the steward arrives in Abraham's old hometown, his first stop is at the town well to water his ten camels. It is evening, the time we are told when the women come to draw water. The steward prays to his master's God, asking for a sign that will reveal who among the women is the right one for Isaac. "If I ask her for a drink and she offers to draw water for my camels as well, that will be the right one."

Before he has even finished this prayer, Rebekah appears. She is beautiful, unspoken for, untouched. And when he asks her for a drink of water, as if on cue she offers to draw water for the camels as well. In fact, the story emphasizes her quickness to oblige. She runs between the well and the trough, filling it several times, since ten camels can drink a prodigious amount. The steward watches her, impressed. When she has finished, he rewards her labor handsomely with a gold nose ring and two gold bracelets. Then he inquires if there might be room at her father's house for him and the ten camels.

Rebekah, ever eager, assures him of a welcome at her home and introduces herself in the customary way by sketching her familial connections. The steward is bowled over when he hears that she's actually his master's great-niece.

Rebekah runs home to tell her mother's household to prepare for a guest. When her brother Laban sees the expensive gifts the steward has already given his sister, he is eager to host this wealthy traveler. He hurries to the well to urge the steward to accept their hospitality.

In typical Middle Eastern fashion, a meal is spread before the steward, but, not wanting to profit from their generosity under false pretenses, he refuses to eat until he discloses his mission. Carefully crafting his message, he outlines Abraham's history since he left Haran many years ago, stressing how his wealth has grown; then he states his present mission—to find a wife for Abraham's son. He reports his prayer that the right girl be revealed to him that very day and the amazing way that prayer has been answered. "Now," he ends, "tell me how this strikes you. I need to know if you are open to my proposition before I take advantage of your hospitality."

Laban and his father practically fall over one another in their eagerness to give Rebekah to this ambassador from their wealthy relative. "Take her; she's yours," they say, adding, "this is obviously divine intervention. Who are we to stand in God's way?" No one, of course, asks Rebekah herself.

Next morning, the steward is anxious to be on his way with his prize. Laban and his mother try to cajole him into staying another week or so—Laban, no doubt, in the hope of extracting more gifts from this guest. But the steward insists he cannot tarry. He is anxious to return with Rebekah so that his master can see the success of his mission before he dies.

In order to stall a bit longer, they decide to ask Rebekah her preference, probably expecting that she would want time to prepare for the journey. Rebekah's reply no doubt surprised them all. "Let's go," she says, as eagerly as she offered to water the camels. So she and her maids mount their camels and follow this strange man from the fertile valleys of Mesopotamia southeast into the unknown.

It would have been many days and miles later before they spotted a man walking alone in a field. He looks up at the approaching caravan, shading his eyes. "Who's that?" Rebekah asks the steward.

"My master," he replies.

Immediately Rebekah makes her camel kneel and slides from the saddle, pulling her veil to cover her face. Her new master is there too, this man who will be her husband. Little did she know that he would prove so easy to manage.

Up to this point, every scene in this story has been presented dramatically, but the narrator draws a curtain across the culmination of this proxy love story. We are told that the two are married, that Isaac loves her, and strangest of all, that he brings her "into the tent of his mother Sarah,"[1] who is long since dead. Had Isaac kept the dwelling as a relic of his beloved mother? Was it a kind of shrine to him? Certainly it held some special meaning for him since this scene ends with the line: "and Isaac was comforted after his mother's death."[2] Rebekah has become the mother-substitute for her new husband. And among the matriarchs, she will be the only woman who does not have to compete with other wives.

That does not mean, however, that her life will be without shadows. For one thing, it takes her twenty years to get pregnant. Though that's considerably less waiting than her mother-in-law Sarah endured, for a Middle Eastern woman it was an interminable tribulation. So her husband Isaac appeals to the Lord on her behalf and she finally conceives.

Then the trouble starts. There is such warfare in her womb that she goes to inquire of the Lord, probably from a local oracle, just what's happening to her. As the first woman in the Old Testament to take this task upon herself, Rebekah is again showing her initiative.

And the Lord answers her: "In your womb are two nations of people. One day they will be separated. One nation will be stronger than the other. It is the older who will serve the younger."

Sure enough, she delivers what at first appears to be a double blessing—twins. But even as infants the boys are very different. The first emerges red and hairy. The second is born with one hand gripping his brother's heel. And that's when the trouble begins.

The first son they name Esau, or Red. The second is named Jacob, or Grabber. And the boys tend to live up to their names. Red is the outdoor type who spends his days hunting. His younger brother is described as "a quiet man"[3] and a homebody. Appreciating the company of women. A considerable consolation to his mother. Their father Isaac, on the other hand, who has an appetite for wild game, relishes the fruits of his older boy's hunting skill.

Jacob, whose own skills lie in the kitchen, is simmering a stew one day when his brother comes in from the chase, sweaty and hungry. "Give me some of that and be quick about it," he ordered in a peremptory way. "I'm starving!"

Jacob, perhaps irritated by his big brother's lack of manners, decides to exact a price from the big lunk. "Fine," he replies, "I'll trade you the stew for your birthright."

"Sure, sure," Red says, brushing him aside. "I'm about to die anyway. What good would it do me then?"

But Jacob suddenly is not kidding. He means it. "Swear?" he says.

"Okay, okay. Just give me some." And he grabs the stew from his brother, muttering something about who needs it anyway.

And now we see that Grabber lives up to his name. He has snatched from his brother the double portion of the wealth the older son would have inherited from their father. Strictly speaking, however, there has been no actual deception. It was a tradeoff—not exactly an even trade, but the terms were clearly stated.

Note that, so far, Rebekah has not been a part of this scheme. Though she is sometimes portrayed as the mastermind behind a conspiracy to supplant her older son with her own favorite, Jacob obviously has no trouble coming up with the idea all on his own.

When Esau reaches forty, he decides it's time to marry. And the local Hittite girls suit him fine. No sense sending away hundreds of miles when you can see what you're getting right there in Canaan. His parents may have disagreed about their two boys, but about these two daughters-in-law they were in complete accord—the two women gave them nothing but grief.

By now, Isaac is old—close to the century mark, in fact—and blind as well. Sensing the end approaching, he knows it is time to give his eldest and favorite son his patriarchal blessing. He calls in Esau and says, "Son, get your bow and arrows and go rustle up some of that wild game you know I love so much. I may not have another chance to eat so well before I die. After I'm full, maybe I'll give you my blessing."

Now it just so happens that Rebekah is in the wings listening to this conversation. Knowing her husband's condition, she would be expecting this blessing ritual to take place soon. She hurries off to find her own favorite son. "Bring me two little goats from the flock. I can fix them so they'll taste like wild game—just the way your father likes it. Then you can serve it to him and get the blessing before your brother gets back."

Jacob hesitates. After all, he's already obtained his older brother's double inheritance rights. Why should he care about the old man's blessing? "It'll never work," he tells his mother. "For one thing, my skin is smooth, not hairy like Esau's. As soon as

Dad touches me, he'll know it's not Red. Then I'll really be in trouble. It won't be a blessing I'll get; he'll put a curse on me for trying to trick him like that."

Rebekah, however, is fully aware that the blessing is much more valuable than property. After all, God had personally promised her that her younger son, her own dear boy, was his choice too. That this sweet, sensitive baby of hers will end up dominating that big oaf Esau. "Not to worry," Rebekah assures him. "I'll take care of everything. In fact, I'll stake my life on it. If the plan doesn't work, let your father's curse fall on me. Just do what I tell you. And be quick about it."

While Jacob is out separating two young kids from their mothers, Rebekah rummages through Esau's clothes and finds his best outfit. When Jacob returns she puts it on him and uses the skins from the goats to cover his neck and hands. After the meat is done, she hands him the platter, and he carries it into his father, pretending to be Esau.

No sooner has Jacob grabbed the blessing rightfully belonging to his brother than Red appears, fresh from the hunt, thrusting his own steaming dish under his father's nose. But it's too late. The blessing has already been spoken, and no matter how loudly Esau protests, it cannot be recalled.

Esau, of course, is understandably infuriated with his younger brother. "Just wait," he mutters to himself. "Dad can't last much longer. As soon as he's in his grave, then I'll get that little wimp Grabber."

But Rebekah has her spies among the household servants, one of whom happens to hear these muttered threats and tells the mistress. As always, however, Rebekah takes the initiative. Jacob may be sharper than his big brother, but she knows he won't have a chance if it comes to a physical confrontation. After thinking it over, she decides she can now actually kill two birds with one stone. She has a new scheme whereby she can not only put the apple of her eye beyond the reach of his brother's murderous schemes but also ensure that he marries well.

Rebekah goes to her husband, who seems unaware of her part in the recent deception, and says with a heavy sigh, "You know, Isaac, life hasn't been worth living ever since Red married those Hittite floozies. What if Jacob does the same thing? I'll just die."

This speech has exactly the effect she intends. Right away Isaac calls Jacob in and orders him not to marry any of the local girls. "In fact," he says, "now that I think about it, the only thing for you to do is to go back to Padan-Aram to your Uncle Laban's. You can't find better women anywhere. That's where your mother came from, after all. Since you're now going to inherit the land God promised your grandfather Abraham, you need to get busy populating it."

So Jacob heads north, toward his mother's people and a land his father has never seen. Rebekah watches her darling go, glad he'll be out of harm's way, confident he will find a better wife among her own people than these dreadful Hittite women. The plan is unfolding, just as God promised before the boys were born. Like the younger son in fairy tales, her Jacob will turn out triumphant in the end, she's certain.

But there's a price to pay: Rebekah will never see her boy again.

Without question, Rebekah engineered this consummation of the plan. Without her conniving, Isaac would have done the customary thing—blessed the eldest son. Was Rebekah truly a manipulative woman, or merely expediting the outcome God had already announced to her during her tumultuous pregnancy?

Certainly she was a woman who never simply sat back and waited for things to happen, unlike her more passive husband. From the first time we see her at the well, she moves and acts with alacrity. But can deception of one's husband be justified by claiming partnership with divine planning?

The text offers no moral judgment of Rebekah's actions. She is neither condemned nor praised for scheming to supplant her older son with her own favorite. We only see the results—and that they were ordained long before her strategizing was conceived.

The entire saga of the patriarchs is full of tales of trickery, some instigated by men and some by women. Did the ancient Hebrews applaud the quality of shrewdness that allows the weak to win out over the strong? Did the original audience for this saga value the quiet Jacob who relied on his wits above the brute force of Esau? Certainly that pattern recurs often in the Old Testament. David and Goliath, Moses and Pharaoh, Elijah and Jezebel are only a few examples of stories that pit the weak against the powerful. Should

Rebekah be stricken from the list? These are questions to ponder, while remaining cautious of hasty pronouncements based on our own cultural conditioning.

Yet despite any uncertainty as to proper judgment of this woman's actions, the one solid lesson we learn from Rebekah's story is that God often accomplishes his goals by unlikely means. As Rebekah's grandson Joseph will later explain to the brothers who sold him into slavery, "You intended evil, but God intended good."

Your Response

1. a. What do you like about Rebekah?

   b. What don't you like?

2. Can you identify with Rebekah in any ways? Explain.

3. Just as Rizpah was powerless to prevent her sons' deaths, so Rebekah was (or at least believed she was) powerless to win Jacob a blessing by direct action. In both cases, men (a king or a husband) were in the driver's seat. How would you compare Rebekah's way of functioning within a constricted role with Rizpah's way?

4. What do you suppose would have happened if Rebekah hadn't manipulated Isaac in order to get the blessing for Jacob?

5. What's the difference between being shrewd in dealing with people and being manipulative?

6. Did/do your parents have favorites among their children? If so, how did they show it?

7. a. Ask your husband, children, or a coworker whether they have observed you manipulating them or others. (Try to resist manipulating them into saying no!) Don't be afraid to ask a nonChristian coworker; he or she might be fascinated to learn you're in a group of women discussing manipulation.

   b. Plan to report your findings to your group at your next meeting. Did you hear anything that surprised you?

A Response of Prayer

8. Take a moment of silence to ask God to let you know it if you are in the habit of manipulating people. Ask him to point it out to you when you do it.

More Manipulative Women

The book *Daughters of Eve* also includes the stories of Delilah and Salome.

NOTES

1. Genesis 24:67, NIV.
2. Genesis 24:67, KJV.
3. Genesis 25:27, NIV.

8
JEZEBEL
Political Women

1 Kings 16:29–19:18, 21:1-29; 2 Kings 9:30-37

Jezebel's Story
EXCERPTED AND ADAPTED FROM *DAUGHTERS OF EVE*, PAGES 180-189.

*I*srael never really took to monarchical government. For one thing, monarchies are usually hereditary, whereas Israel had always relied on the hand of Providence to appoint—and anoint—leaders. Thus Israel's kings, starting with Saul, the first one, were always vulnerable to military coups. But perhaps more importantly, Israel had a higher authority than even the king, one that reached farther back into its history—the Law. While other Middle Eastern monarchs could operate despotically, in Israel no man superseded the Law, not even the king. Kings were mortal; the Torah was eternal. It served as Israel's hedge against absolute tyranny, providing legal protections to every citizen not even the king could disregard.

It is this aspect of Israelite politics that Jezebel never understands. She has grown up in the royal household of Sidon, a city on the Mediterranean coast south of what is now Beirut. As king, her father wields absolute power. When she marries Ahab, son of Israel's king Omri, she fully expects to exercise the same kind of power there that she formerly enjoyed in Sidon.

Jezebel has also grown up in a very religious household. Besides king, her father is also a priest of Baal, the Palestinian fertility god. Introduced into Israelite society generations earlier by some of Solomon's wives, Baal cults already flourish in her new kingdom. Her husband Ahab, a dabbler in Baal-worship himself, offers no objection when Jezebel imports her own favorite goddess Astarte, the female consort to Baal.

For obvious reasons, fertility deities most often came in pairs. Their worship included the physical reenactment of the gods' cosmic coupling, which supposedly brought fruitfulness to fields and flocks. Astarte's temples were stocked with priestesses who played the part of the goddess, receiving the seminal offering of male worshipers—who were expected to make cash donations as well. In special emergencies or community disasters, these gods required the sacrifice of children, often by burning.

Jezebel finds her father-in-law Omri to be quite an able leader, at least militarily. A hundred years after his death the Assyrians still called Israel "the land of Omri." He also built Samaria the new capital of Israel. Ahab and Jezebel live in the palace he erected there, but Jezebel can see that Omri's son fails to live up to his father's mark. Soon Jezebel is setting the tone for Ahab's kingdom, one based on luxurious self-indulgence and sacralized eroticism.

But she overlooks Elijah, the champion God has chosen to combat the Astarte invasion. And the Lord couldn't have picked a less appealing fellow—uncouth, crabby, and often cowardly. Like John the Baptist in a later age, Elijah lives in the wilderness on a diet that would gag most people—bread scraps and roadkill regurgitated from ravens' mouths, morning and evening. While hired prophets are swilling wine back in the palace, Elijah drinks runoff in the wadi.

Then a drought settles over the land. Israelites may have been copulating religiously at Astarte's temple, but the promised fruitful fields have not materialized. Just the opposite, in fact. Because no rain falls to water the crops, the country is facing famine. Soon there's not even ditchwater for Elijah to drink. So the Lord sends him—of all places—to Sidon, Jezebel's homeland. When Elijah reaches the village of Zarephath, he notices a poor widow gathering sticks for a fire. In exchange for her hospitality throughout the years of the famine, Elijah works two miracles for her, including raising her son from death.

Why is this nameless woman introduced in the middle of Jezebel's story? Because the widow's extreme poverty and remarkable graciousness toward Elijah serve as a foil to the queen's opulence and arrogance. Though the widow comes from the same Sidonian culture as Jezebel, she is able to transcend that background and grasp the Living God. She is not culturally bound. Even the women who worship Jezebel's goddess can escape their own degradation and the destruction of their children when their hearts are open.

Jezebel's, however, is decidedly closed. So is her mind. Not content with importing her own Astarte cult into Israel, she now intends to stamp out rival religions, especially that of Yahweh, the Living God. To that end, she has ordered the summary execution of all prophets of Yahweh. The royal butler, Obadiah, has managed to save a hundred such men by hiding them in a cave and smuggling bread and water to them.

Meanwhile, the famine grows worse. There has been no rain for three years now. When Ahab sends Obadiah out to search the countryside for grass to feed the horses in the royal stables, the butler comes upon Elijah returning from Sidon.

At Elijah's request, Obadiah brings Ahab out to meet with Elijah. "Aha," the king says when he sees the prophet, "you're back to stir up more trouble, I see."

"I'm not the troublemaker here," Elijah counters. "You're the one who turned your back on the Law and took up with your wife's gods. But I have a plan. I want you to send for those four hundred and fifty prophets who serve Baal and those four hundred Astarte priests Jezebel feeds. Have them come to Mount Carmel. And tell all the people to come too. It's going to be quite a show."

Ahab is so desperate to end the famine at this point that he complies. The people and prophets assemble at Mount Carmel, a high hill near the border of Sidon. From that promontory Elijah makes a speech to the people. And as usual, he's not very diplomatic. "Why can't you Israelites make up your minds? If Yahweh's in charge, then follow him. If Baal's in control, then make him your only god."

But his challenge meets with nothing but silence.

"Fine," Elijah says. "It looks like I'm the only one left willing to stand up for the Living God while Baal has four hundred and fifty men backing him. But I've arranged a little scientific

75

experiment here. I've got two bulls, one for them and one for me. We're going to cut up the carcasses and lay the pieces on some firewood I've brought. Then we'll see which god can light a fire under this barbecue."

Not surprisingly, despite their frenzied dancing around the sacrifice for hours, the prophets of Baal can't light a spark. Rubbing their nose in their failure, Elijah thoroughly soaks both his firewood and the carcass. With a flash, it goes up in smoke. The people begin to cheer and chant "Yahweh is God, Yahweh is God"—which in Hebrew sounds much like Elijah's own name. Then they lead the defeated Baal-prophets off to their execution.

The prophet's next assignment is to break the three-year drought. Hearing the rumble of thunder in the distance, Elijah tells Ahab to get ready for a downpour. Then he prays: "Please, God, send the people rain." Finally a small cloud can be seen out over the sea. It grows, darkening as it heads toward land.

"This is it," Elijah tells the king, "the rain you've been waiting for. You better get your chariot down off this mountain pronto so you won't get stuck. It's going to be a gullywasher!" Ahab, for once, listens to the prophet and heads back to the Pass of Jezreel.

Elijah is ecstatic. *I'm on a roll now*, he thinks, and hitching up his skirts, runs all the way to the mountain pass, beating Ahab's chariot there.

Meanwhile back at the palace, Jezebel has heard about the massacre of her Baal-prophets, and she's furious. The results of the contest have impressed her not a whit. She sends word to Elijah: "You can bet your bottom shekel that before another day passes you'll be in the same shape as my slaughtered prophets."

So Elijah takes off running again, this time in a different direction. Knowing Jezebel to be a woman of her word, he takes his bodyguard and heads south, skirting the capital. He doesn't stop till he reaches the Negev desert where he holes up in a cave.

Jezebel's temper is not improved when the prophet slips through her hands a second time. Her husband Ahab is not in a good mood either. *Maybe I should encourage him to take up a hobby,* she thinks, *something that would take his mind off all these complicated matters of state.* A little gardening perhaps. Wholesome recreation, fresh air, exercise. That should improve his spirits.

From the palace high on the hill of Samaria the royal couple can look down into the fertile valley of Jezreel, full of vineyards, flourishing now that the drought has ended. Spotting a likely one, Ahab goes down to negotiate a price for the vineyard adjoining his palace property. But Naboth, the owner, isn't interested in selling. "Look," Ahab tells him, "I'm willing to pay a fair price. Or even make a trade, if that's what you want."

"Sorry," Naboth says, refusing to budge, "but it's not a matter of money. This property's been in the family since the Lord divided up the Promised Land among the twelve tribes."

So Ahab slouches home and crawls in bed. "Nothing ever works out for me," he pouts, turning his face to the wall and refusing to eat his dinner.

Jezebel comes in to see about him. "Aren't you hungry, sweetheart? Tell mama what's wrong."

"It's that farmer," the king replies. "I offered to pay him for his dumb old vineyard, but no! My money's not good enough for him."

Jezebel sits back in amazement. "And you call yourself a king?" She shakes her head. "That's not how kings behave, my dear. I'll show you how to take care of this little matter! Now eat your supper and you'll feel better." And she hurries off to write a letter to the city council of Naboth's hometown: *It has come to my royal attention that a farmer by the name of Naboth has been heard making threats against my royal person and cursing Yahweh. This kind of behavior cannot be countenanced inside my kingdom. I decree that you shall detain this Naboth and hold a solemn fast, at which time his accusers will appear to make formal charges.* Then she signs the letter with Ahab's name and seals it with his signet ring.

The city council, who live in fear and trembling of the queen, know who is behind this scheme. They immediately arrest Naboth and arrange for his trial. Meanwhile, Jezebel hires two criminal types to testify that they heard the unfortunate farmer threaten the king. Also that Naboth spoke of Yahweh in a most disrespectful manner. (Jezebel thinks this last accusation is an inspired touch of irony.)

With the hired witnesses against him, Naboth doesn't stand a chance. As soon as the trial is over, the city council imposes the punishment prescribed for such a crime—death by stoning. Then they send word to Jezebel that her wishes have been carried out.

When Ahab hears that Naboth is dead, he gets out of bed and hurries down to Jezreel. His darling Jezebel has been as good as her word—she's acquired the vineyard for him. (The property of convicted—not to mention executed—felons reverted to the state.) Though he's not anxious to inquire too closely into the circumstances, he is eager to take possession of the dead man's vineyard.

But who should be waiting for him at the garden gate but his old nemesis Elijah. "What are *you* doing here?" Ahab asks in shock. "You're always spoiling everything!"

"The Living God sent me," Elijah responds. "Why else would I risk coming back? The Lord has a message for you. And you're not going to like it. It goes like this: *You've sold out, Ahab. And now you're going to have to pay. Not only you, but your sons. There won't be any of your heirs left to claim your throne when you're gone. You let Jezebel and her gods take over my people. She's not off the hook either. And her death won't be a pretty sight: the dogs will gnaw her bones down by the ravine where they stoned Naboth.*

Now Ahab is really depressed. And Yahweh-prophets continue to dog his footsteps. On the eve of a war against Assyria, one of them predicts this will be Ahab's last battle. Hoping to outsmart this prophecy, the king puts on the uniform of an ordinary soldier, but the disguise doesn't work. Ahab is shot by a stray arrow. When they bring his chariot back to the city to wash it out after the battle, stray curs gather round and lap up Ahab's blood.

Nevertheless, Jezebel still wields power as queen mother in Samaria. During the next eight years she continues to work at stamping out worship of that Living God who gives her nothing but grief. Politically, however, the kingdom is falling apart. Finally, an army captain named Jehu revolts, threatening to take over the country. When the new king tries to negotiate, Jehu replies, "What peace can there be so long as that witch Jezebel prostitutes our women in Astarte's temples?" Jehu defeats the king's forces, fittingly enough, in the very field that Jezebel conspired to steal from Naboth.

Back at the palace, the queen hears the news that Jehu has defeated her son's army and is marching toward Samaria. Instead of hiding or trying to escape, Jezebel goes to her room, takes out her cosmetics, and applies her makeup for the last time. Then she fixes her hair elaborately, as if for a state occasion. When she sees Jehu approaching, she leans out the window of her ivory palace and taunts him. "Perhaps you've heard of Zimri, that other peasant upstart who overthrew his master?" she screams down at him. "Well, just remember what happened to him. He didn't last, and neither will you."

Jehu looks up at Jezebel. He sees not only the painted, aging queen, but the shadowy figures of her attendants shrinking in the shadows. "This is your last chance to save yourselves," he calls out to her servants. "If you're on my side, throw Jezebel down and nothing will happen to you."

Immediately, a couple of eunuchs, who no doubt had experienced their share of the queen's imperious cruelty, grab her and heave her out the window. When Jezebel hits the pavement, her blood stains the walls of her ivory palace and even splatters Jehu's horse. He rides right over her mangled body and up to the palace gate.

Later, after a hearty meal inside, he gives orders that the body be taken up and properly buried. "After all," he says, no doubt thinking of his own newly acquired royal status, "she was a princess." But when the servants go out to recover the body, it's too late. The dogs have already devoured the corpse, just as her old enemy Elijah predicted they would. And no one intervened to salvage the body from desecration, a telling sign of how unpopular the queen was among the people.

For three decades, Jezebel had exercised authority in Israel, perhaps even more than her husband Ahab. But she used that power despotically. Neither her religion nor her politics supplied her with any notion of community or a leader's responsibility. Thus her obvious intelligence, talent, and even courage were wasted in the service of cosmic eroticism.

Your Response
1. What did Jezebel fail to understand about:

Yahweh's character?

The way Yahweh viewed political power?

2. a. For what goals did Jezebel use political power?

    b. What was wrong with those goals?

3. a. What were some of Jezebel's methods for achieving her goals?

    b. What was wrong with those methods?

4. Can you think of any women today who are using political power well? Who are they, and why do you approve of their use of power?

5. Can you think of any women today using power like Jezebel? If so, who are they? Why do you liken them to Jezebel?

6. What's your own personal attitude toward political involvement?

A Response of Prayer
7. Pray for women you know of who are politically involved. Ask God to give them a clear understanding of his values, goals, and methods.

More Political Women
The book *Daughters of Eve* also includes the stories of Esther and Herodias.

9
SAPPHIRA
Business Women

Acts 4:31–5:11

Sapphira's Story
EXCERPTED AND ADAPTED FROM *DAUGHTERS OF EVE*, PAGES 205-210.

*A*ccounts of the fledgling church in Jerusalem during its first heady days and weeks have always inspired Christians, especially those of us becalmed in the doldrums of affluence. Prosperity buffers both our society and our churches from the thumps and bruises befalling most of the world's population. But prosperity also puts a barrier between us and the kind of living-on-the-edge elation that ignited the early Church.

Lest we think that this risky life was an easy choice for those first Christians who had little to lose anyway, the Bible supplies us with the story of Sapphira and her husband, Ananias. In order to understand their story, however, we need to look at the post-Pentecost living arrangements of the Jerusalem church.

Peter, having overcome the cowardice he displayed when he denied knowing Jesus after his arrest, is becoming a powerful preacher, and he and John, his old fishing buddy and sometime rival, are performing miracles of healing. Even being jailed and threatened by the authorities does not dampen their boldness.

This daring of these leaders infects all the new believers, now numbering in the thousands. Their inspiration welds them into a body acting with a single will. Barriers of class and origin suddenly dissolve before the rushing tide of the Holy Spirit. Peter and John, for instance, are perceived as "unlearned and ignorant"[1] by the council of priests and elders examining them. We know they have abandoned their occupation and family connections, which leaves them virtually penniless. In fact, their poverty is emphasized when they stumble across a beggar at the temple. "Silver and gold have I none," Peter tells him, "but such as I have give I thee."[2] Then he takes the beggar's hand, helps him to his feet, and heals him by invoking the name of Jesus.

But impoverished or not, the apostles are the acknowledged leaders of this new community. Meanwhile, members who are landowners or householders don't hesitate to sell those assets and turn the profits over to the apostles in order to provide for the entire body.

People who have never experienced this kind of reckless joy may find such intemperate behavior difficult to credit. Yet it occurs periodically, if not frequently, in human history. Sometimes the results are good, sometimes disastrous. The Plymouth Colony of pilgrims operated in much the same mode, as have any number of religious groups in this country. And in the 1960s and 1970s, bands of hippies all over America, sometimes in cities, more often in rural settings, experimented with communal living. A group called Jesus People USA still live this way in Chicago, sharing their income and expenses.

From the description of the early Church that closes the second chapter of Acts, it appears that the people gave up their day jobs to spend most of their time together, either at the temple reveling in their newfound faith or listening to the apostles tell them about this Messiah who had been raised from the dead. When they got hungry, they went to a fellow member's house and ate together. Simple as that. There seemed to be little point in holding onto their money. What good would Roman currency do anyway when Jesus descended from the clouds again, bringing his legions of angels with him this time?

But the early Christians in Jerusalem were not the only communal group in Palestine at the time. Nor were they the only ones awaiting the arrival of a new world order. South of Jerusalem, down along the western coast of the Dead Sea, in the most unlikely spot for a self-sustaining community, lived the Essenes, a monastic community of Jews, mentioned by both Jewish and Greek historians. We know them today as the scribes of the Dead Sea Scrolls, hidden for centuries in caves pocking the bleached cliffs. To preserve the purity of their religion from the corrupting influences of religious and regional politics, the Essenes had withdrawn about 175 BC to this barren stronghold as a sign of their belief that God would one day turn it into a new Garden of Eden when he vindicated those Jews who remained truly faithful. Like John the Baptist, they saw themselves as "preparing a way in the wilderness" for the advent of the Messiah.

Neither ignorant nor uneducated, they had communal living down to a science. Whereas the harum-scarum fellowship of Jerusalem Christians lived hand to mouth on the voluntary contributions of its members, the Essenes had written rules and regulations—and severe penalties for breaking them. One of the Dead Sea Scrolls, "The Community Rule," set forth the mandates for membership, among which was one requiring new members to "bring all their knowledge, their abilities, and their wealth into the community of God, that they may purify their knowledge in the truth of the statutes of God, and may order their abilities according to his perfect ways and all their wealth according to his righteous counsel."[3] An "overseer" administered the funds of their common treasury. For their daily life, the scroll prescribes: "Together they shall eat, together they shall pray, and together they shall take counsel."[4]

Unlike the new Christian community, however, the Essenes were strictly stratified by rank. Refusing to recognize a member's superior rank was a major offense. The Essenes lacked the democratizing tendency of the early Church that welcomed all comers, regardless of social status, physical infirmity, national origin, occupation, or gender.

Among the Jerusalem community of new believers is a man called Joseph, a Jew from Cyprus, obviously one of its wealthier members. He owns a parcel of land that he sells, then brings the proceeds and lays the money at the feet of the apostles. For this act of generosity, they call him "Son of Encouragement."

Perhaps it was this public recognition of an outlander that prompts Ananias and Sapphira to dream up their scheme. Whatever their motivation, the Bible makes clear that they are in this together. Like the Cypriot, they own some property, which the story emphasizes they jointly decide to sell. But they also mutually agree to keep back a portion of the proceeds. Perhaps they received more for their land than the Cypriot did and thus can match the amount of his gift and still have some left over for themselves. So they bring the sum they've agreed on and lay it at the apostles' feet, pretending that, like Joseph's, their gift represents the entire sum they received. After all, who wants to be runner-up in this giving game? Thus Sapphira is partner with her husband both in the sale of property and in the deception.

Peter, however, smells something fishy. Keeping secrets is difficult in such a tight-knit community. When he discovers that the pair have misrepresented their actions, as the community's leader he must confront them about their deceit. Otherwise, the spirit of this emerging community will be compromised.

"Ananias," he asks the man, "how could you do such a thing? Lying to the Holy Spirit like that? Did Satan put you up to it? The property was yours to do with as you liked. No one forced you to sell it or make a contribution. And even after you sold it, you were under no obligation to donate the proceeds. How could you even dream that you could get away with such a lie? It's not me you've tried to deceive or even the rest of the community, but God."

When Ananias hears their scheme exposed in this way, he's overcome—whether by shame or remorse we don't know. All we see is the result: he keels over dead. Had he been an Essene, Ananias would also have been ritually cursed and cast out of the community. But Peter utters no such malediction against this fallen brother. What happens instead is that some young men of the community wind the body in a shroud, carry it out, and give it a decent burial.

That's not the end of the story, however. Later in the day Sapphira returns to the community's gathering place, probably a private home. No one has told her of her husband's untimely death.

"Sapphira," Peter says, "tell me again how much you sold that land for?"

Without hesitation, she repeats the same false figure the couple had earlier agreed on.

"How could you two conspire to do such a thing?" Peter responds. "Didn't you know who you were dealing with—trying to trick the very Spirit of God? You hear those footsteps in the hall? That's the young men coming back from the cemetery where they've just buried your husband. Now they've come for you."

Sapphira collapses. The young men come in, find her dead also, and take her body out to bury beside her husband. Partners in business, partners in crime, partners in death.

This strikes us, just as we are told it did the members of that community, as a terrible story. Their original joy was chilled by the fear this event engendered. The couple is stricken, not by Peter, but by their own guilt.

But in a backhanded way, this incident makes a positive point about women. It confirms that they are indeed responsible as individuals for their conduct. As a partner in this business venture, Sapphira is held to the same standards of accountability as her husband. Neither she nor Ananias are allowed to point the finger of blame at the other as Adam and Eve did. In fact, Ananias never speaks at all, only Sapphira. Each is given an equal chance to confess the deception individually. And their individual failures bring the same results. Sapphira is not let off the hook by being portrayed as the victim of her husband's scheming. If nothing else, this story made clear to women in the early Church as well as to us that they—and we—are responsible for our own moral choices. In fact, immediately following this tale of deception, Luke's record emphasizes for the first time that "multitudes *both of men and women*"[5] became believers.

Your Response

1. Imagine witnessing the confrontation between Peter and Sapphira. How would you feel after that?

2. What did Sapphira value? What was important to her?

3. What do women today do to appear more spiritual than they are?

4. All of us are involved in business, including those of us who manage homes and families full time. What kinds of ethical temptations does your business present to you? (Are certain unethical practices common in your line of work? If so, what are they?)

5. Do you think God struck Sapphira dead? Explain why you think that.

6. Why do you suppose people who lie to God today rarely drop dead?

7. What do you think God wanted the church to learn from Sapphira's example?

A Response of Prayer

8. Take a brief time of silence to ask yourself these questions:

- Am I trying in any ways to appear more spiritual than I really am? How?
- Am I doing anything unethical in my work or home management?
- If I answered yes to either of these questions, what should I do next?

9. Allow a moment for silent prayer. The leader can then close by asking God to reveal any hidden sin among you.

More Business Women

The book *Daughters of Eve* also includes the stories of Rahab and Prisca.

NOTES
1. Acts 4:13, KJV.
2. Acts 3:6, KJV.
3. Michael A. Knibb, *The Qumran Community*, vol. 2 of *Cambridge Commentaries on Writings of the Jewish and Christian World 200 B.C. to A.C. 200* (Cambridge, England: Cambridge Univ. Press, 1987), page 79.
4. Knibb, page 113.
5. Acts 5:14, KJV; emphasis added.

10
THE NECROMANCER
OF ENDOR
Women and the Supernatural

Leviticus 20:27, 1 Samuel 28

The Necromancer's Story
EXCERPTED AND ADAPTED FROM *DAUGHTERS OF EVE*, PAGES 220-224.

*K*ing Saul has his back to the wall. His kingdom is crumbling, running through his fingers even as he tightens his grasp on it. Internally, his people's confidence in him is ebbing. Externally, the Philistines are eating away his borders. Bouts of madness exhaust his spirit. Even though Jonathan, his heir, still fights by his side, the king knows his son despises him. And just when Saul needs him most, Samuel, the prophet who has always counseled him, deserts him by dying.

Tomorrow Saul knows he must fight what may prove to be his last battle. The Philistines have made deep incursions into northeastern Israel. They are camped at Shunem, within sight of Mount Gilboa, where Saul's troops sit waiting for his orders. Only the Valley of Jezreel lies between the two armies. What will happen to his kingdom if Saul is defeated tomorrow? He already knows the galling answer to that question. That upstart David is waiting in the wings to take over. The kid Saul took under his wing years ago when the boy killed the Philistine giant. For several years now, ever since Saul chased him off, David has been gathering all the malcontents from Israel for his own army, even hiring out as a mercenary for Saul's enemies.

The future has never looked so bleak for Saul. What should he do? Fight or flee? Before he died, Samuel warned him that the spirit God sent to Saul when he was anointed king had been recalled. He spoke the truth. Saul has felt its absence for some time now. When he implores the Lord to speak to him directly, only silence answers. He's already tried flipping a coin, rolling dice, even having his dreams analyzed in order to get some hint of what will happen tomorrow. Nothing. The prophets he pays to advise him don't come up with anything either. Only Samuel had the kind of access to God Saul needs now. The future is nothing but a blankness. Worse than knowing the worst is knowing nothing at all. If only Samuel were still around.

Then Saul gets a last, desperate idea. Earlier in his career as king, back when he'd still been God's fair-haired boy, in a fit of moral earnestness he had issued orders outlawing wizards and necromancers who conjure up the spirits from the region of death. That kind of dabbling in the spirit world is dangerous, Saul knows. But then so are the Philistines. There must be some medium left in the land somewhere, willing to come out of retirement this once and arrange a séance with Samuel. He's the only person, living or dead, that Saul trusts to tell him the truth about the future.

So the king confers privately with a couple of his trusted men. "I need a medium," he tells them. "Go find me one."

It doesn't take long. "There's one living in Endor," they report.

Unfortunately, the town of Endor lies on the far side of the Philistine army. The trip there will require both courage and cunning. Saul disguises himself as a common working man in case they are captured. Then, under cover of night, he and his men slip out of his tent, down the valley, and past the enemy encampment. They have to make their way in the dark over eight miles of rough terrain to the bluff where the town sits. Below, the cliff's walls are pocked with caves. The woman who can conjure spirits from the dead probably lives in one of them.

Though she is often called "the witch of Endor" in later literary references, the woman does not change people into toads or perform magic tricks like witches. She is a "medium," sometimes called a "spiritualist" today. That is, someone who makes her consciousness available to an intermediary spirit, known as her "familiar," who contacts spirits of the dead for her.

The men call out to the woman, and when she appears, she's understandably suspicious of these strangers skulking in the shadows. "I need you to do something for me," one of them says. "I want you to use your powers to call up someone from the Pit. Someone I've got to talk to."

The woman stares at the stranger incredulously. "You've got to be kidding. That kind of thing's against the law. You know what the penalty for conjuring spirits is? I gave that up long ago." She squints at him sharply. "Are you trying to make trouble for me?"

But the stranger persists. "Look," he says, "I've got friends in high places. I swear nothing will happen to you. Just do it, okay?"

So, reluctantly the woman goes about her former business of contacting her "familiar" to communicate with the world of the dead, the place the Hebrews called "the Pit." The Scripture reports the event straightforwardly. Though it provides no details about the paraphernalia and ritual of necromancy, it nevertheless treats the exercise as a reality. And the lady delivers the goods.

"Who do you want to talk to?" the familiar spirit asks, using the medium's voice.

"Call up Samuel," the stranger says.

It is not until the woman sees a figure rising from the ground, a shape no one else can see, that she recognizes the prophet and puts two and two together. She begins to shriek, turning on the stranger. "You're the king, aren't you? Why didn't you tell me? You've tricked me!"

"Don't worry about that," Saul says, brushing aside her anxiety, "just tell me what you see."

"It's like—I don't know—a god rising out of the earth."

"What does he look like? Tell me, tell me," Saul prods her.

"Well, let's see. He's a real old man. And he has on this mantle kind of thing."

Realizing that the prophet, though invisible to him, is amongst them, Saul drops to his knees, bowing his forehead to the ground.

"Why have you troubled me, summoning me from the depths?" demands the ghost of the prophet in a truly sepulchral voice.

"I'm in a terrible mess," Saul cries. "The Philistines are attacking. God has disappeared. He won't talk to me. Not in my dreams, not through my prophets. That's why I've called you up. You've got to help me. Tell me what to do, Samuel. I'm desperate."

And Samuel tells him all right. More than he really wants to know. Tomorrow the Philistines are going to win what will be the final battle for Saul and his sons.

At that news, the king collapses, overcome both by terror and weakness. (He's probably fasted in preparation for the séance.)

Seeing the shape Saul is in, the woman drops her occult role as medium and becomes very practical. "Don't blame me," she tells the prostrate king. "Remember, I only did what you asked me to. I've trusted you with my life. Now if you'll just listen to me, I can at least get you on your feet again. What you need is a good hot meal. Let me fix you something and then you can be on your way."

At first Saul declines. "No, no, I'm fine. Just leave me alone."

But his men agree with the woman. "Come on, chief. We'll help you to the bed over here where you can rest while she's fixing you a snack."

A snack, indeed, she thinks, and hurries off to kill a calf. While that's roasting, she mixes up some bread dough. There's no time to wait for it to rise. It'll have to be flat bread, probably like pita. When the midnight repast is ready, she brings it to the men and watches them eat, no doubt amazed at such a turn of events. A king, eating supper in her bedroom!

But by tomorrow night, this man will himself be among those very spirits he commanded her to call up tonight.

Though this woman plays only a bit part in this contest of kings, and we never hear of her again, she is an oddly likable creature. Unlike Shakespeare's witches, she is not depicted as a snaggle-toothed crone who decorates with skulls and cooks with eye of newt. She renounces her occupation as a medium when it is outlawed and only takes it up again under royal pressure. No one even offers to cross her palm with silver during the transaction. And when Saul swoons after his encounter with the underworld, she sensibly, even generously turns to a practical, physical remedy for his feebleness.

In fact, if Saul, like this woman, had accepted the changing circumstances of life, if he had retired from his former career as gracefully as she did, he would not have felt the need to countermand his own laws. And he might never have had to fight that final disastrous battle.

Your Response

1. What do you make of this story? (Did Samuel really appear? Was it a demon pretending to be Samuel, or was it a hoax? Is it possible to contact dead people via an intermediary spirit?)

2. Why do you suppose the biblical account presents this woman so matter-of-factly, without expressly condemning her as a terrible person?

3. Three thousand years after these events took place, people around the world still try to call up dead people through intermediary spirits. Whoopi Goldberg won an Oscar for portraying a medium in the film *Ghost*. What do you think is the appeal of this practice of spiritism?

4. a. Can you identify with the desire to talk to someone who is dead? Explain.

   b. What about the desire to know the future? Can you identify with that? Why?

5. What has been your own experience with the supernatural, if any?

6. In 2 Samuel 28:7, Saul specifically requests a woman who is a medium. He says it as though most or all mediums were women. Why would this be a particularly feminine line of work?

7. Leviticus 20:27 prescribes death for mediums. Why is being a medium so terrible?

8. Look back over the ten sessions of this study. What have you learned? What will you take with you?

A Response of Prayer
9. Thank God for what you have gained from this study. You might give each group member a chance to thank God for one thing she has gained.

More Women and the Supernatural
The book *Daughters of Eve* also includes the stories of Huldah the prophetess and Mary Magdalene.